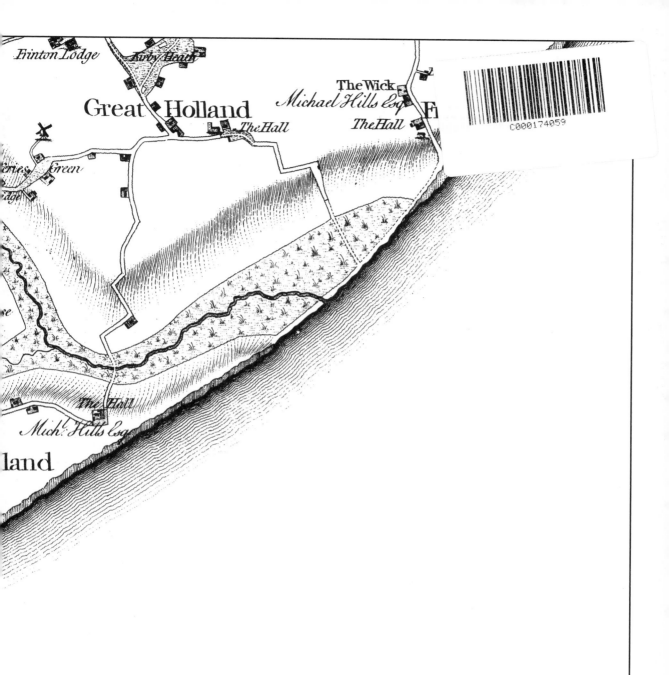

Detail from the 1777 Chapman & André map of Essex, depicting Clacton and surrounding area.

CLACTON
PAST

with

Holland-on-Sea and Jaywick

A 1950s publicity shot showing Clacton's West Beach, the pier and the pleasure boat, Nemo II.

CLACTON
PAST

with

Holland-on-Sea and Jaywick

NORMAN JACOBS

Phillimore

2002

Published by
PHILLIMORE & CO. LTD.
Shopwyke Manor Barn, Chichester, West Sussex

© Norman Jacobs, 2002

ISBN 1 86077 225 0

Printed and bound in Great Britain by
BIDDLES LTD.
Guildford, Surrey

Contents

List of Illustrations

Frontispiece: 1950s publicity shot

Acknowledgements

FIRST AND FOREMOST, I would like to acknowledge the debt I owe to Kenneth Walker, the author of *The History of Clacton* and innumerable articles about Clacton in various magazines and journals. Kenneth has kindly put at my disposal all the fruits of his own research, as well as discussing this book with me and giving me many pointers and much constructive criticism. Secondly, I would like to thank Roger Kennell for allowing me to use his book *From Little Holland to Holland-on-Sea* as the main focal point of my chapter on Holland.

The illustrations in the book are reproduced by kind permission of:

Leo Bentley, 48, 70; Clacton and District Local History Society, 20, 21, 24, 25, 26, 27, 29, 32, 35, 40, 59, 65, 66, 72, 80, 85, 89, 90, 91, 92, 93, 94, 97, 99, 108, 124, 129, 130, 131, 140, 149, 150; Roger Kennell, 55; Pearl Lonsdale, 78; the late Vi Stewart, 81; Tendring District Council, frontispiece, 100, 101, 135, 137, 138, 139, 141, 145, 146, 147, 152, 154, 157; Harry Thompson, 133, 134; Peter Underhay, 9, 84, 96; Ken Walker, 10, 11.

Illustration no.1, the Clacton spearpoint, is © The Natural History Museum and is reproduced with their kind permission.

I

Prehistoric Clacton

PREHISTORIC FINDS from Clacton were first reported in 1831 when John Brown, an amateur geologist from Stanway, reported finding fossil bones on the beach and in the cliffs at Clacton. These finds were followed in 1861 by the Rev Osmund Fisher of Elmstead, who reported finding a fossil deer horn which showed signs of human working. But it was in 1898 that the possible importance of Clacton's place in the history of human development first came to the attention of archaeologists when Rev Kenworthy, the vicar of Braintree, exhibited a collection of fossils and 20 Stone-Age axes found at Clacton at a meeting of the Essex Field Club.

In 1911 an amateur archaeologist called Hazzledine Warren began an investigation of Clacton's beaches and cliffs to see what further evidence of prehistoric human habitation he could discover. Warren's investigations lasted for 40 years and were to unearth finds which were to establish Clacton as one of the major prehistoric sites in Europe. In fact, Warren hit upon one his most important discoveries in his very first season when he came across a wooden spearpoint buried in the cliffs below the Palace Theatre. At first he thought it was the antler of a deer, but it turned out to be a piece of yew wood that had been roughly fashioned and fire-hardened into a thrusting spear. Until recently this tool, about 15 inches long and one and a half inches in diameter was the earliest known man-made wooden artefact to have been discovered anywhere in the world, dating back some 400,000 years. In 1997, however, radiocarbon dating confirmed that three wooden spears found at Schöningen in Germany dated to roughly the same period and may even be a little bit older. The German discovery was important in proving that

1 *The wooden spearpoint found by Hazzledine Warren in 1911. It is approximately 400,000 years old and one of the four earliest known human-made wooden artefacts in the world.*

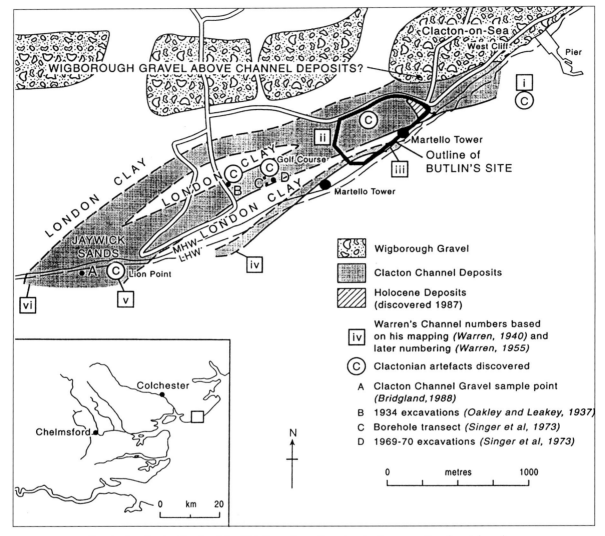

2 *A plan showing the site of the Old Stone-Age settlement and where excavations have taken place.*

the Clacton find was not just a chance one and confirmed that spears were probably being made in large quantities, thus proving that these people were probably hunters and not just scavengers.

The people who made this spear had settled in the Clacton area during the Hoxnian inter-glacial period some 420,000-400,000 years ago on the banks of a river which at that time flowed through Clacton on a roughly semi-circular course between what is now Edith Road to Clacton golf course. The Hoxnian inter-glacial followed the Anglian glacial period, the coldest recorded, when the most southerly ice sheets reached as far as the River Stour. At that time Britain was still joined to the continent of Europe so there was no North Sea and the river on which the Clacton settlers set up camp was the River Thames, which at that time flowed on a more northerly course through Clacton and into Europe where it met the River Rhine.

Riverbanks were ideal places for settlements as they provided fresh water and meat as animals came to drink at the water's edge. From the bones found in the area we can tell what sort of animals were caught and eaten by these early Stone-Age settlers in Clacton. They included giant oxen, bison, red deer, fallow deer, pigs, rhinoceros, horses, straight-tusked elephants, lions, beavers, voles, mice and woolly mammoths. As yet no human remains have been found so that, apart from the animal remains, evidence for the settlement comes in the form of man-made objects, the spear and hundreds of hand-worked flint tools.

There has recently been much controversy about the place of Clacton's flint tools in the evolution of 'man the tool maker'. The earliest tools now generally accepted as man-made are known as Oldowan tools and come from Africa. They date back to something like two to two and a half million years ago. These tools were very crude. A big advance in tool making came about one million years ago, also in Africa, when a more advanced type of human known as Homo Erectus appeared. He began a new method of making tools which became known as the Acheulian industry. The most characteristic Acheulian tool was the handaxe, a large pear-shaped implement, much more refined than the old chopping tools of the original African Oldowan industry. These tools were originally made by using another large stone to strike the target stone or by flaking against a stone anvil (a very large stone). Later on more advanced techniques were used which involved shaping using wood, bone or antler. The Acheulian industry spread to Europe about 700,000 years ago.

The flints found at Clacton, however, are different to either the old Oldowan industry or the more advanced Acheulian tools and form a group all of their own and are known only from a few sites in southern England and northern France. So unique are they that the style to which they belong has been given the designation Clactonian industry. The main emphasis of the Clactonian industry was on removing flakes from the main core of the flint by using a hammer technique and then working on the flakes to make sharp tools for scraping hides, cutting meat and working wood, while using the core left behind as a chopping tool. Clactonian man did not make the pear-shaped axe so indicative of the Acheulian industry.

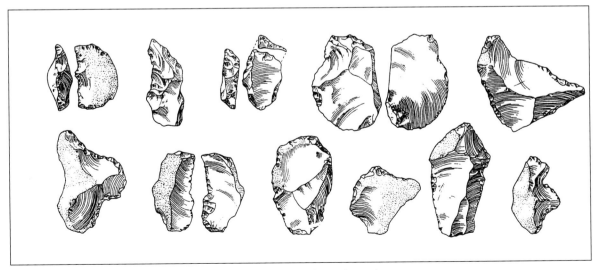

3 *A selection of Clactonian flint tools, mostly scrapers.*

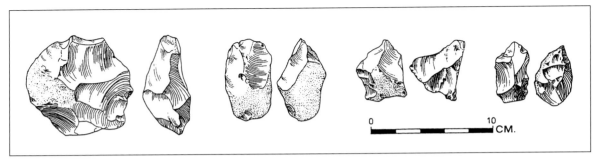

0   10
CM.

4   *A selection of Clactonian flint cores.*

Until comparatively recently it was thought that the evidence from Clacton showed it to be the earliest site of human habitation in Great Britain. However, the discovery of well-made Acheulian type hand-axes at Boxgrove in the 1980s in deposits pre-dating those at Clacton put paid to that theory. Since then other older Acheulian industry tools have also been discovered. At first this seemed a bit curious, as it appeared that the Clactonian tools were more primitive than the Acheulian tools and should therefore be older. But careful study of the Clacton flints shows that a consistent technique was in operation and that the main emphasis was on creating smaller scraping tools by a method known as alternate flaking, which was a way of making as many scrapers as possible from one large flint core. Although there was no attempt at making a well-made hand-axe shape, there was a definite practical method and technique in operation for making the best possible and most economical use of flints to hand, so the makers were perhaps not as primitive as first thought and it may be that there is no difference between the people who made each type of tool.

In addition, recent discoveries at sites such as Swanscombe in Kent and at Little Thurrock in Essex have shown Clactonian and Acheulian tools in the same deposits. It is even the case that six hand-axes were recovered from the foreshore at Lion Point in 1985. The issue of Clactonian v. Acheulian is still a controversial one in archaeological circles and it is true that there is no firm evidence that the Acheulian finds from Swanscombe, Thurrock and Clacton were made by the same people as made the Clactonian tools. One day maybe we will know for sure but, unfortunately, with the growth of Clacton, it is now almost impossible to hold further archaeological excavations along the old riverbank. Perhaps the last chance came in 1987 when Butlin's was being

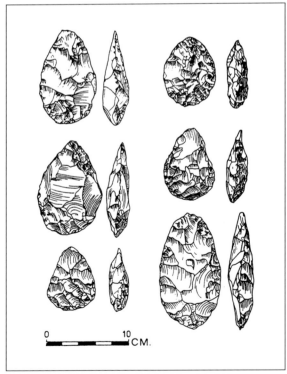

0   10
CM.

5   *A selection of Acheulian hand axes from Swanscombe and Dartford in Kent.*

demolished and a team led by John Wymer investigated the site.

One other point of interest about the Clacton site is that the concentration of material so far discovered over a distance of three kilometres from near the pier to beyond Lion Point is unique in Europe.

Clacton also had a neolithic (New Stone-Age) settlement as pottery remains, known as Mildenhall-style pottery, dating back to c.3600-3100 BC, have been found at Lion Point.

The bulk of neolithic material dug up at Clacton, however, comes from the end of the period, c.2000-1700 BC. Again it was Hazzledine Warren who first discovered this material. Whilst working in the Lion Point area in 1936 he came across a large scattering of potsherds and flints which he recognised as neolithic. He also discovered evidence of a campsite with cooking-holes and hearth sites. On these he found worked flints, pot boilers, charcoal, bones and burnt earth showing evidence of campfires.

Most important amongst all his finds, though, were the pieces of pottery of a very distinct type, later given the name of Grooved Ware or Rinyo-Clacton Ware. This type of pottery was later found to be typical of late neolithic pottery in Essex. Although all the pottery recovered by Warren came from Lion Point, he found neolithic flints scattered over a distance of two to three miles west of the pier. Altogether he recorded 522 flints from the foreshore, the majority being scrapers but there were also some arrowheads, knives, borers, cores and flakes. Because of its national importance, Warren gave the collection to The British Museum.

The next recorded settlement in the Clacton area was well on into the Iron Age after the Celts had arrived from Europe during the last century BC. They were split in to a number of local groups with the most powerful in north Essex being the Catevellauni, who established their capital at Colchester. Rivers were very important to these people as a means of travel, particularly in Essex which was heavily wooded at this period. It is likely, therefore, that the Celtic inhabitants of Colchester would have followed the course of the River Colne down to what is now St Osyth. As the sea was vital to these people, because it meant access to the continent for imports and exports, they would probably have looked for a safe harbour which they would have found just to the north at a large estuary which formed the mouth of Holland Brook.

Between St Osyth and Holland Brook these Celts discovered a spur of land bounded on three sides by streams, perfect for defensive purposes and for providing fresh water for themselves and for animals, and with a rich soil ideal for planting their crops. With close access to the sea and the river route back to the capital at Colchester, it was the ideal place for a settlement. We now know that spur of land as Great Clacton and it is from this time, just over 2,000 years ago, that we can trace, albeit tenuously in its early days, the development of Clacton-on-Sea.

Unfortunately, there is no record of what the Catevellauni called their village, but it is thought they settled in or cultivated the whole of the surrounding area as far away as Jaywick. It is known they had a pottery manufacturing site at Bull Hill, near the site of the present day Co-op Fiveways supermarket. Colchester Castle Museum has one of the beakers made at this pottery. Celtic gold coins have also been found on the beach at Clacton. These were probably used to trade with the Roman Empire on the continent of Europe. These links were put to good use when a Belgic tribe known as the Trinovantes ousted the Catevellauni from Colchester. The Catevellauni appealed to the Romans for help and the Emperor Claudius, looking for any excuse to expand his Empire, immediately invaded Britain which, following the Romans' victory, became a province of the Roman Empire.

II

Medieval Period

FOLLOWING the Roman occupation of Britain Colchester became an important administrative centre, but after its destruction around AD 60/1 by the Iceni queen Boudicca it lost its importance and was rebuilt as a sort of retirement town for old soldiers known as Colonia Claudia Victrensis. It is known that the Romans enjoyed the pleasures of the seaside and it is therefore certainly possible that Clacton Beach enjoyed an existence as a seaside resort during this period. In 1897 two Roman urns were discovered near the beach when the *Grand Hotel* was being built and other Roman remains, including coins, have been found at various locations around Clacton including Holland Road, in the present hospital grounds and on Vista Road Recreation Ground.

There is also some evidence to suggest there was a small Roman settlement at Great Clacton as Roman tiles can be seen in the walls of the present St John's Church. It was common for Norman builders to use Roman tiles, left over from ruins of old Roman buildings in the neighbourhood. What that building, or buildings, might have been is open to speculation as nothing has ever been found apart from the tiles in the church. It is also fairly certain that Roman soldiers would have been sent from Colchester to patrol Clacton Beach. This part of the English coastline, with its flat sandy beaches, was particularly vulnerable to attack from the conti-nent and there is no doubt that throughout much of the period of the Roman occupation attacks on the coastline by Saxon pirates and warriors increased in intensity.

When the Romans finally left Britain in AD 410 the whole of this area was left at the mercy of the Saxons, and by the end of the fifth century the East Saxons were in control of an area roughly equating with the present day Essex, with London as their capital. The well-defended area originally settled by the Celts on the spur of land between St Osyth and Holland Brook became an attractive site for a small group of East Saxons who settled the area and continued the Celtic tradition of farming the nearby land. The leader of this band in all probability was a man called Clacc, and it is from him that the name Clacton derives. Originally known as Clacc-inga-ton, the name means the estate of Clacc's people.

As well as arable farming, Clacc's people were able to use their ready access to the sea to set up saltings and fishing areas, while the local marshes provided excellent pasture for sheep, which in turn provided the Saxons with milk and cheese. These dairy farms were known to the Saxons as wicks, and there are still a number of places in the area with the name wick to remind us of their origins, including Wigborough Wick (belonging to a man called Wicga), Cockett's Wick and Jaywick, which was Clacton's own dairy farm. Very little evidence remains of these early Saxon settlers although there is some evidence of a Saxon cemetery in West Clacton on the old Butlin's site (now Martello Bay).

In the seventh century Vikings attacked the coastal settlements of Essex. It is not known for sure whether Clacton suffered at the hands of these Scandinavian marauders, but it is from this time that the story of St Osyth dates. St Osyth was said to be the wife of Sighere, the King of Essex, but it is thought that following his reversion to paganism Osyth left him and turned to the Church for comfort, building a nunnery in the neighbouring parish of Chich. When the Vikings invaded this part of the coast they are said to have assaulted the nuns, but Osyth stood up to them and they cut her head off. She is then said to have run to the church clutching her head as she ran. Her martyrdom led eventually to her being canonised and a priory built in her memory. Whether any of this story is actually true or not is another matter. Nevertheless, it is almost certainly the case that Vikings did raid this part of the coast in the seventh century and indeed continued to do so through until as late as the 12th century.

It is also probably the case that some Vikings settled in the area and there is some evidence to suggest that they were the first to build sea defences on the marshes west of Clacton. During the seventh century the East Saxons were converted to Christianity and it is possible, though again uncertain, that a small chapel was built on the site of the present St John's Church. Essex itself came under the diocese of London with St Paul's Cathedral owning most of north-east Essex. Being so close to the sea, Clacton may well have become the centre of a profitable sea-borne trade between London and north-east Essex.

The first recorded mention of the name Clacton in an official document dates from the year 1000, when Claccingtune was required to contribute two men towards a ship's crew. There is a further mention

6 *St John's Church, Great Clacton, was built in the early 12th century by Richard de Belmeis, the Bishop of London and lord of the manor of Clachenton. The walls were six feet thick and probably intended as a refuge in times of trouble.*

7 *The interior of St John's Church, Great Clacton. The nave and chancel both date from the 12th century. The three bays of the nave are divided by wide pilaster buttresses which suggests that the roof was formerly vaulted.*

of the name shortly after the Norman Conquest, when William I granted the manor of Clackinton to the Bishop of London. It is not clear whether this meant Clacton came within the Royal Forest at that time, though this could be inferred from a later writ of 1216 which stated, 'that by the King's charter free warren was granted for ever to the Bishop of London and his successors in the Manor of Clackinton and that of Walton-cum-Thorp. Also that they had full liberty to take stags and hinds, and all sorts of wild animals within the limits of the said Manors.'

By the time of Domesday Book in 1086, 45 tenant farmers and 50 smallholders occupied

Clachintuna. There were also five knights, with two villeins, 45 smallholders and three serfs between them. In total, the population of Clacton, which would have included both Great and Little Clacton, was about 550. Domesday also reported that Clacton contained woodland for 400 pigs, pasture for 100 sheep and had 20 acres of meadowland. However, in spite of all this land there was actually only one cob, seven head of cattle, 30 pigs and 41 sheep.

In 1108, Richard de Belmeis became Bishop of London and therefore lord of the manor of Clacton. He took a close personal interest in the area and shortly after his appointment visited Chich (St Osyth), 'which at that time formed part of the domain of Clachenton, where he had a house'.

It was almost certainly de Belmeis who was responsible for building St John's Church in Great Clacton, although its original dedication has been rendered as St Nicholas. The church he built was a fairly substantial building for such a small village and it is probable that de Belmeis constructed it for use as a refuge in times of trouble as well as for worship, giving some credence to the idea that Viking raids had not totally finished off this part of the coast. The walls were over six feet thick and would have provided an effective defence against any attacking enemy, whether from sea or land.

At this time Clacton was one manor and the name Great Clacton, as distinct from Little Clacton, does not appear in the historical record until 1286. However, it is probable that the separation into two separate parishes dates from de Belmeis' time as he was also probably responsible for the building of Little Clacton's parish church of St James. Belmeis gave the new church at Great Clacton to his monastery at St Osyth, so the monks collected the tithes and appointed the vicar, probably from amongst their own number. They also owned the nearby manor of Canon's Hall (Cann Hall).

As well as being a keen builder, de Belmeis appears to have been a keen huntsman, enjoying the

8 *St Osyth priory was yet another of Richard de Belmeis' buildings. It was erected in the early 12th century to commemorate the martyrdom of St Osyth.*

9 *The Ship Inn, built c.1500 right at the end of the medieval period. The annual midsummer fair, which dated back to the 12th century, was held in the square in front of the Ship.*

Royal Charter which allowed him to hunt deer on his Clacton estate. Not being satisfied with the old local park, he enclosed a large area of wood and heath between Clacton and Thorpe known as Clacton Park. Alton Park to the west of the modern town may well be a corruption of de Belmeis' original land known as 'Old Town Park', its name also surviving in Alton Road, Park Road and Park Way.

De Belmeis' house and that of successive bishops of London probably stood near St John's Church. In the fields to the north of their residence was a large fishpond, while near the present Valley Road was their vineyard. The subterranean passages beneath the old village may date back to this time. One passage runs from the north side of the church towards St John's Square and others are reputed to have entrances at Great Clacton Hall, the *Ship Inn*, the *Queen's Head* and at Eaglehurst, the house next door to the *Ship*. There has been much written about these passages, many writers subscribing to the romantic notion that they were used as hiding places by smugglers, but they were probably nothing more than the bishops' drains.

The residence fell into disuse early in the 15th century and some of its materials went into building the church tower which replaced an older wooden belfry at this time. It is probable that the tower was intended to be a massive structure and a landmark for sailors out at sea, but the Abbey's finances were not up to the expenditure needed and the work was never completed. Today the tower is capped by a weatherboarded belfry.

During the Middle Ages it is probable that the only regular visitors to the windswept beach lying at the foot of the low rugged cliffs were the monks of St Osyth, who would have continued the Saxon tradition of fishing. Remains of their activities have been found on the beach in the form of pieces of pottery dating from the 12th to the 15th centuries. In fact, this area was so rewarding for the monks that it became known as 'Fortune of Plenty'. There may also have been occasional trips to the beach by the villagers following especially heavy seas in the hope that there might have been a wreck or two and the cargo washed up on to the beach. This was a particularly dangerous activity, not only because of the weather and the state of the sea, but also because William I had issued a charter proclaiming that the lord of the manor was entitled to all such wrecks. If the lord found that any of his villagers had got there first he did not hesitate to remind them of his rights. For example, villagers were once fined 53s. 6d. for taking a small ship which had a cargo of two thousand herrings, and on another occasion a local couple who discovered and took away a chest containing clothes, two periwigs, a sword, two bronze candelabra, two pictures and some books were duly summonsed to appear before the quarter sessions for stealing.

The monks of St Osyth finally lost their hold over the parish during the reformation when Henry VIII dissolved the monasteries. Henry VIII himself became lord of the manor in 1545 and from then on the lordship remained in secular, if not always royal, hands and the village moved on to a new phase in its life.

III

The Post-Medieval Village

AS THE MIDDLE AGES came to an end, and the post-medieval world came to Great Clacton, life continued undisturbed. The rural economy still dominated local life, though the nearness to the sea began to grow in significance over the next couple of hundred years. But, for the time being, agriculture was the mainstay of the village, the chief crops being wheat, oats and barley, with most of the residents employed on local farms as labourers.

For the most part the villagers still lived, as they had done in medieval times, in small timber and thatch cottages spread out in the area around the church, the *Ship Inn* and the *Queen's Head*. St

John's Road, then called simply The Street, would have been a muddy lane with water being obtained from nearby wells which, in all probability, were very polluted. An epidemic in 1615 killed 35 people in the village, about one-tenth of the population.

The midsummer fair, dating back to the 12th century, was probably the highlight of the year. By the 18th century the date had been set to coincide with St Peter's Day, 29 June, and the fair would have been home to itinerant pedlars offering everything from sweetmeats to toys and fairings, as well as the travelling showmen who would have set up their swingboats and roundabouts. It was eventually

10 *A drawing by Clacton historian Kenneth Walker giving some idea of how the* Queen's Head *public house would have looked during its heyday in the Napoleonic period.*

Great Clacton Street   K. Walker

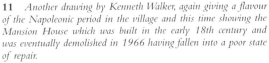

The Former Mansion House, Great Clacton   K. Walker

11 *Another drawing by Kenneth Walker, again giving a flavour of the Napoleonic period in the village and this time showing the Mansion House which was built in the early 18th century and was eventually demolished in 1966 having fallen into a poor state of repair.*

12 *One of Clacton's Martello towers, built between 1810 and 1812. This one, at the foot of Tower Road, is the only Clacton tower to be moated with a drawbridge.*

abolished in 1872 following reports of vandalism and unruly behaviour.

St John's Church continued to dominate not only the religious life of the parish but also its temporal affairs. Once a year, at Easter, the village elders would meet in the vestry to elect officers for the coming year, decide on what rates to levy and discuss other important matters. The officers appointed were two churchwardens, two overseers of the poor and two surveyors, who were responsible for the maintenance of the roads. Although the village set its own rate, this had to be endorsed by a Justice of the Peace, who also had to satisfy himself that the village accounts were in order.

By far the biggest burden on the village finances was the poor. All paupers were a charge on the parish where they were born, so 'foreign' poor were quickly chased out of the village. In fact great efforts were made to avoid having any paupers around at all. At least three families were sent − all expenses paid − to Canada, while in another instance, a detective was hired to search for a man who had left his family so that he could be made to uphold his financial responsibilities.

Some of Great Clacton's accounts can still be seen in the Essex Record Office and these record what the money was spent on; for example, a stumacker, a lemmon, pudding bags and a neck of mutton for 3d. There is also one entry which reads 'To Bumbo 6d'. In the 18th century a local farmer was paid £21 a month to provide all necessities for the poor of the parish, including '3 good hot dinners of wholesome butcher's meat every week, and on other days to provide them with cold meat and good and wholesome bread and cheese, and with good wholesome beer.' Some of the more wealthy inhabitants sometimes made generous bequests to the poor. In the 16th century, for example, some almshouses were endowed in Magdalen Green, on the site of what is now the *Coach and Horses*.

However, the village also possessed its dreaded workhouse on the corner of the present London Road and Old Road. This was originally a cottage called Red Oaker Hall which was acquired by the parish in 1707. It could accommodate up to 30 inmates, though it is doubtful whether it was ever put to the test, as generally the numbers were far fewer than this. The working day for those poor souls sent to the dreaded institution lasted from 5 a.m. till 9 p.m. in the summer. No-one was allowed to bring 'strong drink or Tea' into the house. This workhouse lasted until 1834, when responsibility was transferred to Tendring and the new workhouse at Tendring Heath.

For those even lower down the social scale, i.e. criminals and prisoners, Great Clacton had its own public cage at the entrance to the churchyard, though apparently this grew so dilapidated that three prisoners managed to escape through its roof. In 1765 a payment was made for 'putting down a new whipping post in ye [work] House'. One particularly sensational case occurred in the village in 1635 when George Burges was hanged for murdering his wife, Susan. During the 17th century five women from Great Clacton were imprisoned for being witches following an investigation by the infamous Witch-Finder General, Matthew Hopkins. This was in 1645. Kenneth Walker speculates in his book, *The History of Clacton*, that Ware Pond, opposite the house called Yew Trees, was used for ducking witches.

At the opposite end of the social scale, Great Clacton boasted a relative of King George I among its inhabitants in the 18th century when Colonel Schutz made his home in Great Clacton Hall. Schutz was a cousin of the king and accompanied him when he came to this country to claim the throne in 1714. In 1717 he paid £6,300 for various properties in Great Clacton including Great Clacton Hall and Cann Hall. He held various positions at court but still found time to immerse himself in the affairs of the village, at one time being a lay rector and an overseer of the poor.

Proximity to the sea brought a new element to the life of the village in the 18th century when it

13   *The Street, Great Clacton. This photograph, taken just before the First World War, still shows a number of buildings dating back to the 17th and 18th centuries. From left to right: The Old Forge, the* Queen's Head *public house, the Mansion House, the old shops, St John's House.*

14 *A close-up view of the old shops which dated back to the 18th century. Before the coming of Clacton-on-Sea this was the village's main shopping centre.*

seemed the whole village was involved in some way or another with smuggling off the desolate coast. In 1728, for example, a reward was offered for the apprehension of a gang of 30 or 40 smugglers who had badly beaten the riding officers and constable who had tried to arrest them, while some years later another gang of 17 smugglers was caught by customs officers, who were themselves then captured by another gang. If the cargo being smuggled were large enough it was not unknown for anything up to 300 men to be involved. One local family involved in smuggling was the Webb family, who traded as butchers in Great Clacton and may at one time have occupied Bennett's Farm in Little Holland.

The *Ship Inn* was possibly a meeting place for the smugglers to transact business with their contacts. Originally built in the early 16th century, it started life as a yeoman's house but became an inn *c.*1709 when it was acquired by Thomas Joy, a victualler.

The earliest mention of its name comes in 1727, when a report of a meeting said it had taken place at the 'sign of the *Ship* in Clacton'.

In 1788 John Cobbold, a brewer from Ipswich, bought a part interest in the inn and 12 years later he bought it outright. It remained in the Cobbold Family for almost 200 years. The other main inn in the village, the *Queen's Head*, dates back to about 1600 and was originally a house called Layes. The first record of the name *Queen's Head* comes in 1679. It was also taken over by Cobbold's in 1844.

The *Plough Inn* was originally the *Queen's Head*'s brewery, while next door there stood a maltings. Another maltings stood at the top of Old Road, then known as Brook Street. There was a forge in Valley Road (Holland Road), a wheelwright's in North Road (Butt Lane) and a windmill in what is now Windmill Park just off Old Road (Brook Street). In the centre of the village in St John's Road (The Street), opposite the *Ship*, were a number of shops sandwiched between the Mansion House at one end and St John's House at the other. The Mansion House, a red brick double-fronted house on the corner or St John's Road and North Road was built *c*.1720 by William Field. The present St John's House dates from the early 19th century but is built on the site of an early 18th-century house originally owned by Thomas Fisher, who sold grocery, drapery and ironmongery.

Somewhere around this time it is probable that local public transport first appeared, with carriers' carts plying between Great Clacton and Colchester, stopping at villages *en route*. They would have carried mainly goods and mail and maybe the occasional passenger. After the railway was built to Colchester, Taster Bagley, landlord of the *Ship Inn*, was advertising a bus service leaving Clacton 'every Tuesday and Thursday mornings at Half-past 7 o'clock, in time for the Parliamentary Up-train leaving Colchester Station at 10.10am; returning from Colchester at those days at half-past Four'.

During the 18th century the *Ship* was the main centre of village social life, but during the 19th century it seems to have been superseded by the *Queen's Head*. This is probably because of the entertainments the landlord laid on during the Napoleonic wars in the early 19th century. At that time the military were passing backwards and forwards through Great Clacton on their way between their barracks at Weeley and the Martello towers down on the beach. The village became a convenient break for the soldiers on their way and many a military thirst was slaked in the *Queen's Head*. The landlord was able to use his new found wealth to rebuild and enlarge the inn by adding an imposing bow window and a ballroom upstairs for the officers, who also had the use of a garden on the opposite side of North Road, which was laid out as a bowling green.

The Martello towers were built as part of Britain's defence against the threat of invasion from Napoleon's France. War had been declared in 1793

and in early 1795 a number of signal towers had been constructed in north-east Essex, including three at Little Holland, St Osyth and Clacton. Two years later four gun batteries were erected in the district, including one at Holland Haven and another at Clacton Wash (at the foot of Wash Lane). Brigadier General Sir John Moore visited the area with Major Hay of the Royal Engineers and his observations made him very concerned at the vulnerability of Clacton to attack. Furthermore, he was worried that any army landing at Clacton would have no difficulty in marching on Colchester and from there on to London. He was most concerned that the area should be properly defended. On 3 July 1797 his fears of an invasion seemed to come true as a French privateer, *Les Graces*, landed near Little Holland having been driven ashore by an English revenue cutter, the *Viper*. Over twenty Frenchmen hurriedly ran up the beach and disappeared before the revenue men had a chance to land. When they did, they immediately raised the alarm and warned the local residents. A messenger was dispatched to seek the aid of the military stationed at Colchester. Word got around that these foreign 'devils' were ravaging the country, committing murder and rape, though of course they were doing no such thing and were probably more frightened than the locals. When a detachment of soldiers eventually arrived at Clacton they were too late, as all the French had been captured by the revenue men and local farmers. Those involved in the capture were rewarded with a night of celebration in the *Ship Inn* and 400 pints of beer, paid for at public expense. Fortunately, in 1798 Bonaparte decided not to invade and the threat receded for a while, especially after the Peace of Amiens was signed in 1802. However, in 1803 war was once again declared and English defensive thoughts returned to the vulnerability of Clacton Beach and its strategic significance. More troops were needed in the area and a new barracks was built at Weeley to become the centre of the defence.

15 *Magdalen Green was a small hamlet that grew up between the centre of Great Clacton and the sea. It is not clear how it obtained its name, though it may derive from the almshouses established there in the 16th century to house magdalens (or poor women).*

The army had already begun to build Martello towers on the south coast. (The name Martello comes from one of seventy or so circular towers built on Corsica as part of the island's defence against British attacks. One particular tower, known as Tour de la Mortella, had withstood British attacks in 1794 so well that it was decided to copy it for our own defence. Mortella was wrongly reported as Martello in naval despatches of the time.) Because of the strategic significance of Clacton and district it was decided to build a number of towers along this stretch of coast. In all five were built in the area later to become part of the Clacton Urban District. Building commenced in 1810 under the direction of General Whitmore. He was very anxious about their stability as they were built directly on to marshland. He later wrote that the 'soil was of the consistency of butter and when a greater weight was given to one side in the progress of building over the other, the mass of masonry had a tendency to incline on that side.' One tower sank ten feet before it could be finished.

The towers were finished in 1812 and supplies of guns and ammunition despatched from London. The towers were manned by the troops from Weeley but none were actually stationed in the towers themselves as it was felt 'the unhealthiness of the coast would render it inadvisable to place the Troops in the Towers and Batteries.' By 1815 the Napoleonic wars were over and the towers, after just three years, were rendered useless for their original purpose. In 1819 a number of them were pulled down, including the one at Little Holland, but those at Jaywick and the three along Clacton Beach remained and are still standing to this day, all of them having been used for a variety of purposes over the intervening 180 years or so.

With the Napoleonic wars over, the soldiers left Weeley Barracks and for the time being at least Great Clacton settled back to its sleepy rural ways. The corn market continued at the *Queen's Head* and was attended by farmers across the Tendring Hundred. They all sat round a long table to conduct their business with their clay pipes and tobacco

16   *The Windmill. This particular windmill was built in what is
now Windmill Park in the middle
of the 19th century and replaced
the former mill which had been
sited further out from the village
near Foots Farm and was
destroyed during a storm. This mill
did not have a long life and fell
into disuse after its owner, Mr
Charles Beckwith, built a steam
mill in 1867. It grew more and
more dilapidated and was finally
demolished in 1918.*

tins. This market commenced at 7 p.m. on Tuesday and sometimes lasted all night. In fact it was not unknown for the meeting to continue until the following Saturday.

In the mid-18th century the benefits of sea bathing had been discovered by the aristocracy and gradually the whole idea of spending time by the sea became a popular pastime for those with the leisure to be able to indulge in it. Great Clacton villagers themselves began to appreciate the pleasures of a Sunday evening stroll through the cornfields down to the beach. In 1820 a gentleman from Colchester by the name of Sargent Lay visited the area and decided it was perfect and ripe for development. His plans, however, came to nothing. In 1824 the enterprising Taster Bagley was advertising a

bathing machine on the beach 'for the accommodation of those who are desirous of enjoying the benefits of sea-bathing', and in the 1840s a cottage in Rosemary Road was providing refreshments for beach parties.

The scene was being set for the coming of Clacton-on-Sea, but before this came about there was one more major incident affecting the ancient farming community. On 5 December 1830 a crowd of farm workers, including a large number from Great Clacton, gathered near Colchester. The meeting was held to give vent to the farm workers' dissatisfaction over two issues, namely their poor wages and the increasing use of machinery, which was making their skills and therefore themselves redundant. Two days later the Great Clacton workers

17 *Towards the end of the 18th century this farmhouse, known as Pilcroft's, was owned by Abraham Thorp, the same man that owned Sea Side House Farm, on whose land Clacton-on-Sea was later to be built. Pilcroft's farmhouse still stands in Old Road and is now part of Bowen's International.*

took it upon themselves to take action in the matter and set out to smash as much machinery as they could. At least thirty men arrived on John Smith's farm at Alton Park and hacked the threshing machine to pieces. They moved on to Bull Hill Farm, Kiln Barn Farm and to a number of others. In all they smashed up seven machines that day. Later in the day the men had an altercation with the farmers in the village street, but apart from a few threats ('We will have blood for blood', 'We will do for him') there were no reports of actual violence. The following day they moved on to Little Clacton where they broke up a machine at a farm called the Lodge.

On the following Saturday nearly 1,000 farmers and local gentry met at Tendring and rode off to Great Clacton to round up the rioters. One month later ten men from Great Clacton and six from Little Clacton appeared at the County Quarter Session. Six men were sentenced to seven years transportation, while the rest were given sentences of between three and 18 months hard labour. It was to be the last time that farming would take centre stage in the story of Clacton. From now on the story would switch to the coast.

IV

The Beginnings of Clacton-on-Sea

THE GREAT BULK of the land we now know as Clacton-on-Sea belonged to a farm called Sea Side House Farm, which was situated on the corner of what is now Rosemary Road East and Station Road. This was an ancient farm which, in the 17th century, had belonged to a man called Richard Mosse, the chief constable of the Tendring Hundred. During the 18th century it was sold a number of times and by the 1770s was owned by a man called Abraham Thorp, a farmer from Weeley, who also owned Pilcroft Farm in Great Clacton. In October 1779 Sea Side House Farm was acquired by a St Osyth man called William Howard. When he died in 1809 he left the land in trust to his daughter, Elizabeth. One of the conditions of this trust was that the land could not be sold during the lifetime of Elizabeth or her husband, William Watson. It was for this reason that, just at the time when entrepreneurs were looking to buy up land on the coast to turn it into seaside resorts, the area around

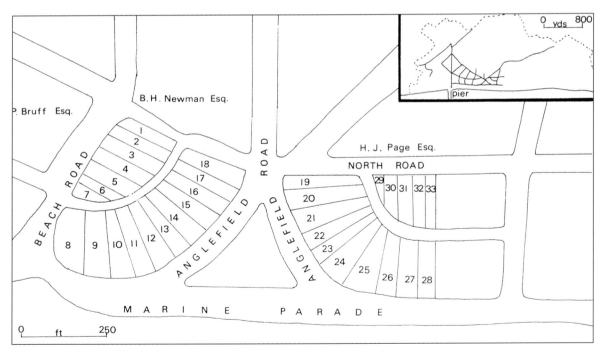

18 *A plan of the Cliff Estate as laid out for auction in 1872. Inset is a map showing the full extent of the development of Clacton-on-Sea at that time.*

Clacton Beach was safe from any such development.

Following the Napoleonic wars the farmhouse itself was demolished but further cottages were erected in Rosemary Lane, and by 1851 there were 11 families living in the area then known as Clacton Beach. These were mostly coastguards or farm labourers.

William and Elizabeth's eldest son, Joseph Yelloby Watson, generally known as J.Y. Watson (and you can understand why!), acquired the *Hotel* in Rosemary Road in 1851 and turned it into his summer residence, renaming it Verandah Lodge. Also about this time, the Watsons bought a new-fangled steam engine for use at Sea Side House Farm to thresh the corn. It was, by all accounts, an awesome spectacle as it belched out great volumes of smoke

and made ear-splitting noises. This new machine was the talk of Great Clacton, and one of the older school of gentlemen farmers from the village rode over to find out what all the excitement was about. He took one look at it, exclaimed 'Sir, it is the Devil!' and then rode off without another word. It came from a new world that was soon to engulf him and his fellow villagers.

Elizabeth Watson died in 1848 and was buried in St John's churchyard. Her husband lived on until November 1864, and with his death the trust conditions ended and the farmland became available for sale and development. J.Y. Watson lost no time in advertising the property for sale and in April 1865 the press carried an advertisement announcing that an auction was to be held in 'June or July next'

19 *Clacton-on-Sea, The New Watering Place, the earliest known representation of the new seaside resort of Clacton. This print was published in* The Times *newspaper to mark the opening of the pier in July 1871.*

had also been responsible for the London to Colchester, Colchester to Ipswich, Ipswich to Norwich and the Norwich to Spalding railways. He had designed the Colne Valley Viaduct and was owner of the *Clifton Hotel*, Walton. He was actively involved in Colchester politics and served on the Board of Improvement Commissioners for Walton, the forerunner of the Town Council. As if all that wasn't enough, he also made time to found the Tendring Hundred Waterworks Company.

At the time Sea Side House Farm came up for sale, as well as building the Walton railway Bruff was investing a great deal of money in promoting Walton as a seaside resort, buying up land, building houses and a public hall, supplying the town with gas and water and shoring up the sea defences. But as soon as Clacton Beach came onto the market Bruff practically dropped Walton overnight as Clacton appeared a more attractive proposition and he saw the potential right away. Four factors influenced him:

1. It was a virgin site with hardly any existing buildings so he could plan it all out as he wished.
2. There was plenty of room for expansion both inland and along the coast. (Walton was very restricted in its development potential due to its siting on a narrow headland bounded by the sea with marshes to the rear.)
3. Clacton was not subject to coastal erosion to anything like the same extent as the more exposed site of Walton.
4. It was near his current railway and he felt it would not take much effort to link Clacton to the line.

at which the 'valuable freehold building land' known as Clacton Beach was to be sold off in lots. The advert went on to mention 'the fine sandy beach', 'the purity of the air' and the 'extraordinary healthiness of the place'. At the bottom of the advert, Watson added that he was willing to discuss the possibility of selling the whole as one lot prior to the auction.

One man who was interested in buying the whole lot was Peter Bruff. Originally from Portsmouth, but by now domiciled in East Anglia, with houses in both Ipswich and Walton-on-the-Naze, Bruff was a civil engineer and currently engineer in chief of the railway line being built from Colchester to Walton (the Tendring Hundred Railway).

Bruff was a remarkable example of the Victorian entrepreneur. As well as overseeing the work on the Walton line, he was also involved with the development of both Walton and Felixstowe as seaside resorts and with civil engineering projects in Colchester, Harwich, Ipswich and Lowestoft. He

Consequently Bruff bought the 50-acre site in 1865 and immediately sought parliamentary powers to construct a railway from Thorpe-le-Soken to a point just 60 yards from the cliffs, together with a 300-yard-long pier. The Thorpe and Great Clacton Railway Act was passed in July 1866, giving Bruff permission to build the railway and pier with the proviso that they had to be completed within five years otherwise the powers would lapse. The Act also laid down a scale of charges for landing goods at the pier, which included 6d. for a barrel of gunpowder, 1d. per cubic foot for musical instruments, 2s. 6d. for turtles and £1 for a corpse!

21 *A companion photograph to the previous one, showing the Royal Hotel in 1872.*

Bruff's proposals to create a seaside town did not go down at all well amongst the village elders in Great Clacton. They were most concerned about the effect this new town would have on their rural peace and calm. At a village meeting just before Christmas 1865 they unanimously agreed to 'dissent from the company carrying on this scheme'. And, just in case anyone was still not clear about how strongly they felt on the matter, they underlined the word 'dissent' in the minutes.

Unfortunately for Bruff, he seemed to be undergoing something of a cash flow problem at this period, and in 1868 the Tendring Hundred Railway Co. called in the receiver so the railway to Clacton never materialised under Bruff. To complete his pier, however, he looked to outside finance and turned to the Woolwich Steam Packet Company. This company was successfully running steamers on the London to Margate route and was looking

for a stopover point about the same distance north of the Thames as Margate was to the south as a way of increasing the trade on their Ipswich route. Bruff arranged to meet their chairman, William Parry Jackson, actually on the windswept and desolate beach at Clacton. We can only imagine how the conversation went and the picture Bruff painted of his new town, but whatever he said it worked, and the Woolwich Steam Packet Company agreed to finance the building of the pier in return for the right of their steamers to call there. In early July 1871 the *Essex Gazette* reported that building was going well and that the pier would be ready to receive visitors within the next couple of weeks. It described the new watering place of Clacton-on-Sea as 'an adjunct to Walton-on-Naze'.

Eventually, the five-year deadline to build the pier was beaten by just two days when, on 18 July 1871, the first steamship ever to call at Clacton landed at the pier. Its name was SS *Queen of the Orwell*. Clacton-on-Sea's official opening as a town

came on 27 July 1871, when the Woolwich Steam Packet Company brought 300 guests on board the SS *Albert Edward* to take part in the opening celebrations. As the pier was only 300 yards long, vessels could only berth during high tide, and the visitors therefore had a limited stay. One couple, however, had wandered too far inland and when they returned to the beach they found that the *Albert Edward* had already cast off. A boat was found to take them out to the steamship but, as they were boarding, the lady fell into the water, apparently much to the amusement of those on board ship. Perhaps it was a symbolic baptism for the new town.

Coincidentally, 1871 was the year the Bank Holiday Act was passed, giving workers the day off on August Bank Holiday. It was a fortuitous start to Bruff's venture of creating a seaside resort, though not perhaps one he personally would have wished for as it was not 'workers' he was after. In fact, while the pier was being built, he had been busy making plans for his new town of Clacton-on-Sea and in July 1871 he published his outline designs.

23 *Pier Avenue, c.1880. On the right in the centre is the Public Hall, one of the undertakings of the Woolwich group of companies, the Clacton-on-Sea Hall and Library Co. Ltd, set up in 1875. On the left at the front are the offices of Clacton's first newspaper, the Clacton Gazette, which was really just a local edition of a Colchester paper.*

Bruff's vision was of a high-class development and to that end his proposals amounted to a few semi-detached villas, hotels and open spaces for recreation and promenades along the cliff. He insisted there would be 'no slums, nor any object that can offend the eye', knowing that it was only property of a reasonably high standard that could provide the rates needed to fund large projects such as sewerage and drainage.

Bruff's lasting legacy perhaps was his 'Deed of Mutual Covenants' which purchasers of individual plots of land had to sign. The deed dealt with items such as standards of drainage, fencing, paving, lighting, etc., and made sure that all these facilities were kept up to the high standard laid down by Bruff. Clacton-on-Sea had suddenly arrived. Newspapers of the time showed how rapid the development was. As early as 1871 local papers were reporting

> A pier has been built at which the Ipswich steamers will call, a roadway has been made through the cliff, and spaces have been marked out for promenades, pleasure grounds, villas, lodging-houses, an hotel, shops, a library, and a bazaar. At present Clacton-on-Sea waits the coming man in the shape of the bricklayer, the navvy, and the carpenter.

And shortly afterwards,

> You can scarcely move but you come upon reminders of the enterprise abroad. Deal planks,

bricks (plain and ornamental), drain pipes (big and little), walls rising a few feet above the ground, improved walks, the nautical flag-staff, ring of trowel, the recurring taps of hammer.

A satirical article in a magazine called *Judy* – a Victorian rival to *Punch* – summed it up when it said, 'Did you ever hear of Crackton – Crackton-on-Sea as it is now? Nobody ever did, I am certain, until a month or two ago. Then all at once Crackton woke up one morning and found itself famous as a "favourite marine resort".'

Although Peter Bruff maintained his interest in the town by becoming a shareholder in the Woolwich Steam Packet Co., direct control for many of its undertakings passed over to the company under Jackson. Their next project was to build a hotel 'in order to induce people to visit the place'. It therefore floated a new company in October 1871 called the Clacton-on-Sea Hotel Co. Ltd. The directors included Jackson and Bruff and the *Royal Hotel* eventually opened on 24 July 1872, just one year after Clacton-on-Sea's official beginning.

Amongst other companies formed by the directors of the Woolwich Steam Packet Company (which as well as William Jackson, included Able Penfold, William Agate, James Ellis and Thomas Hayes, names now familiar to Clactonians as road names in the centre of town) were the Clacton-on-Sea Gas and Water Co. Ltd and the Clacton-on-Sea Hall and Library Co. Ltd. It was at this point that a new name entered Clacton's history, a man called James Harman who became managing director of the Hall & Library Co. Harman was a London solicitor who himself bought up 50 acres of land around Clacton. And by 1876, when yet another new company, the Clacton-on-Sea General Land, Building and Investment Co. Ltd., came into being, its directors, Jackson, Hayes, Penfold, Ellis and Harman, controlled an area of 213 acres, over four times the size of Bruff's original investment.

Whilst the building was beginning on Bruff's original area of land at the centre of Clacton-on-Sea, another small estate was planned to the east beyond Beach Road and centred on Anglefield. The land had been bought by William Grimwade of Hadleigh, Suffolk on 30 December 1871 from the trustees of Charles Gray Round. He had the land laid out by the Colchester architect, G. Gard Pye, as the Cliff Estate and offered it for sale by auction in 33 lots. The Cliff Estate reflected Bruff's influence in the provisions for drainage, the vendors guaranteeing to 'place a pipe drain along the back roads, with a junction, to which the purchaser of each lot could connect to the drains' and the restriction on the types of houses that were to be built. In lots 1 to 7 and 29 to 33, no dwelling house was to be built of value less than £300, lots 8 to 28, no detached house of less that £400, or pair of semi-detached houses of less value than £700. The auction took place in June 1872, but only 18 of the plots were sold. The unsold lots were again offered for sale in 1873.

On 23 May 1873 Grimwade acquired land contiguous to the Cliff Estate from Henry James Page of Thurrowgoods Farm, and over the next two years Page continued to lay out most of his farm as far as Victoria Road for development. For many years the gap in the cliff leading from the end of Victoria Road down to the Marine Parade remained the eastern limit of Clacton-on-Sea.

Between 1872 and 1875 Clacton's development continued steadily. Tenders were announced for six shops with residences and stables and, additionally, a tender was accepted for the erection of a pair of villas and a bazaar opposite the *Royal Hotel*. On 18 September 1875 the *Kentish Independent* reported

telegraph posts ready for erection, a chemist about to start selling drugs … and a ladies school on the front parade. There are bathing machines, donkeys, and Mr Harman has built himself a house far away to the eastwards tempting development in that direction.

24 *Another of the Woolwich Steam Packet network of companies was the Clacton-on-Sea Gas and Water Co. This is a view of their pumping station in Old Road taken in 1895. The diver is preparing to go down and inspect the well.*

25 *The formal inauguration ceremony of the town's first lifeboat, the* Albert Edward, *on 20 July 1878 as recorded in the pages of* Pictorial World. *The day was declared a public holiday locally and thousands of people attended the ceremony. The* Albert Edward *had in fact arrived in Clacton on 12 March and had already been launched on 23 May after the brig* Garland *had run aground on the Gunfleet sands.*

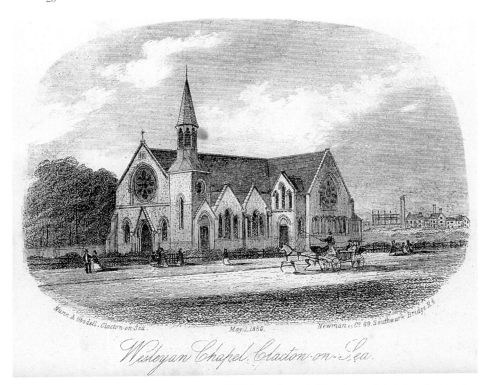

26 *The Wesleyan Chapel, later called Trinity Church, at the corner of Pier Avenue and Rosemary Road, was built in 1877. This print dates from 1880.*

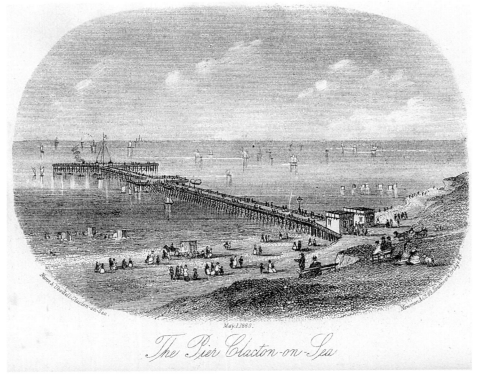

27 *An 1880 print of the pier. This shows the beach before the sea wall was built and before the cliffs were landscaped.*

28   *The sea wall to the east of the pier was built in 1881. This photograph was taken in 1885, the year in which the owner of the* Royal Hotel, *Mr Wallis, opened his Hot and Cold Sea Water Baths at the foot of the pier.*

In 1874 the *Essex Standard* reported that a controversy had arisen between the two major land owners, Bruff and Page, over the siting of Clacton's first church, St Paul's. A committee, which included Bruff, had been set up to consider 'the fact that there was not any provision made for the spiritual welfare of either the residents or visitors'. Bruff offered a good site in the centre of his development together with £100 as a donation towards the building costs. However, Page also offered a plot of land on his development for the building of a church. Harman supported Page and offered to become 'responsible for the larger share of the necessary funds'. When the committee accepted Page's offer, Bruff resigned.

The foundation stone for the new church was laid by James Round MP and the church itself opened in 1875. Clacton-on-Sea became a parish

in its own right in 1878. St Paul's was one of the first buildings erected on Mr Page's latest plot of land and for many years it stood quite alone in the fields. Ironically, in 1890 a mission hall was erected in the High Street because it was felt that St Paul's was too far from the centre of town.

A second conflict also involving Harman arose the following year, 1875, when applications were made by Henry Finer of *Verandah Lodge* and Mr H.J. Simpson of *Osborne House*, both situated in Rosemary Road, for full liquor licences. The applications were opposed by Frederick Mann, manager of the *Royal Hotel*, and James Harman, on behalf of the Clacton Hotel and Pier Co., on the grounds that additional licences would affect the chances of the *Royal Hotel* recouping its outlay expenses as there was insufficient build-up of property in the area to warrant them. Harman added that Clacton-on-Sea was 'being laid out in a manner to render it respectable in appearance, and it was impossible if licences were to be granted that it should continue to be so'. The applicants stated their opposition to the *Royal's* monopoly and also asserted that there was a need for facilities 'of perhaps not so high class'. This controversy proved to be the first challenge to Peter Bruff's idea of Clacton-on-Sea becoming and remaining a 'high class watering resort'. For the moment Bruff's ideals were safe as both applications were rejected.

The census of 1881 showed a population for the new town (excluding Great Clacton) of 651. Shops had been established, including Edwin J. Gilders and Shadrach Sparling, the town's first postmaster, who operated from a shop on the corner of Pallister Road and Station Road. Two further hotels had been established, the *Osborne* and the *Imperial*, both in Rosemary Road. There was also a Public Hall, a small lecture hall and a library as well as a bank, three private schools, two churches, the Trinity Methodist Church, built in 1877, and the Anglican Church of St Paul's. Gas had been laid on to every home, and in 1878 the town's first lifeboat, the *Albert Edward*, had been launched and was housed in the old lifeboat house in Carnarvon Road.

Following Bruff's failure to provide a railway in the early days, a committee was set up in 1876 to examine again the prospects of a railway link, and a proposal was made to link the line to the Tendring Hundred Railway at Thorpe-le-Soken. In 1880 William Jackson laid the foundation stone of Clacton railway station. In his speech he claimed that he 'was the father if not the grandfather of Clacton-on-Sea, and he was, therefore, the most suitable man to select for the laying of this stone'. Bruff received just a brief mention at the ceremony. Dogged by problems of weather, geology, legal issues and even a strike, the opening of the new line was delayed many times, but was finally declared open by the Mayor of Colchester on 4 July 1882. The headmaster of Great Clacton School wrote in his log book that day, 'A great many absent, they went to see the first train to Clacton-on-Sea.' The coming of the railway dealt a devastating blow to Bruff's plans, supported by Jackson, Harman and the rest, of maintaining Clacton's 'high class' image. What the railway did was make it much easier and quicker for Londoners to organise days out at Clacton. It was not just lower middle-class and working-class families who were now able to get to Clacton relatively quickly and cheaply, but there were also pub outings from the East End of London and day trips for orphans and other underprivileged groups organised by churches and philanthropic organisations in the capital. In June 1883 for example, at least four groups of London poor and underprivileged came down on organised outings.

Clacton's image changed almost overnight, becoming the brash, popular holiday resort it was to become noted as over the next century or so. In 1884 visitors wrote to the *Walton and Clacton Gazette* to complain that

> … the Pier, which was always the select promenade of the town, disfigured at its entrance, as I think by a stall … emitting what appeared to be a strong odour of fish. I cannot help thinking this will have some prejudicial effect on this years' receipts as the better class of visitors take a decided objection to such an affair,

and

> Clacton-on-Sea will soon have a painful and even ruinous experience if speedy measures be not taken to stop the present rush of the lowest type of London excursionists – men and women, boys and girls – who seem only to enjoy themselves when they are revelling in drink and obscenity, both of language and behaviour.

Perhaps Bruff too felt he would like to underline the word dissent!

Clacton was about to enter its next phase of development.

V

Victorian and Edwardian Clacton

THE CONFLICT between village elders and new town entrepreneurs came to a head with the proposal to enlarge the Special Drainage District (SDD). This had been inaugurated in 1879 as a local arm of government with the purpose of raising rates to fund drainage and sewerage works within the area controlled by the Land Company. The creation of this high-rated area at the centre of Clacton made land just outside its boundary a better proposition for speculative builders who were now taking an interest in the coming seaside resort. This was especially true of the hamlet of Magdalen Green situated midway between the new town and the old village.

So the Land Company proposed in 1882 that the boundaries of the SDD be enlarged to take in the rest of Clacton. Those outside the present boundary felt this would benefit only the speculators in the central area, while the Land Company argued that it would prevent others from taking advantage of the fact that those within their area were paying higher rates which benefited those outside the area. James Harman complained that 'although their property is nearly as valuable as that within the district … owners were selling land outside the district for very large profits.' The argument was finally resolved in favour of the Land Company and in 1884 the Special Drainage District was extended to cover the whole of the parish of Great Clacton. The resulting election to the SDD Board finished with six of the seven representatives being

from the new breed of entrepreneur, while the four unsuccessful candidates were all members of old Great Clacton farming families.

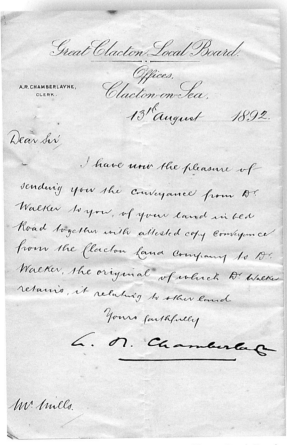

29 *Headed notepaper from the Great Clacton Local Board, 13 August 1892. The Board was inaugurated in 1891 and wound up in 1895, on the creation of Great Clacton Urban District Council.*

With the continued growth of Clacton-on-Sea, Essex County Council agreed that it should form a new local authority area of its own and consequently, on 17 June 1891, the Great Clacton Local Board came into being, taking over all the duties of the Tendring Rural Sanitary Authority, covering drainage, lighting, paving, the approval of new road and buildings, sanitary inspections and the powers to acquire and maintain parks and pleasure grounds.

In 1892 it was agreed to build a new Town Hall to house the new local authority and J. Wallis Chapman was appointed architect. A vacant plot of land on the corner of Rosemary Road and High Street was chosen and building began the following year. The total cost of the building was £12,000 and it included a bank (a branch of Gurneys, Round Green, Hoare and Company, later incorporated into Barclay's Bank), shops and a theatre (the Operetta House) as well as the council offices and assembly

30 *(above)   A view from the top of the water tower, c. 1880, looking out over Pier Avenue. The large field in the centre is where later shops like Woolworth's, Marks & Spencer and W.H. Smith's would be located.*

31 *(above right)   A companion photograph to the previous one, this time looking out over the Wesleyan Chapel (Trinity Methodist Church). To the left of the photograph three paths with posts along them can just be discerned which are obviously being laid out for development. These are Wellesley Road, Hayes Road and The Grove.*

32 *(right)   The plots of land at the corner of Rosemary Road, Station Road and High Street, c. 1891, where the Town Hall was due to be built along with Arcade Buildings. It is possible the boards that can be seen on the two plots are 'for sale' signs or notices about the impending building work.*

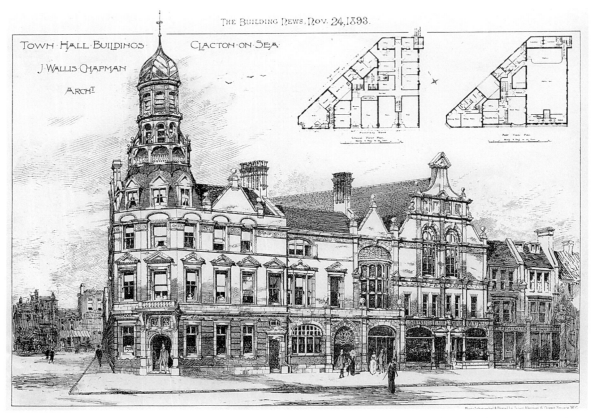

33 *An artist's impression of the new Town Hall Buildings drawn for* The Building News, *24 November 1893 edition. It is a view along the Rosemary Road frontage showing the Clock Tower, bank building, offices, the proposed Operetta House and two shops to the rear. Ignore the view behind the building to the north!*

rooms. The whole was topped off by a fine new town clock. The opening ceremony was performed on 4 June 1894, although the offices had been occupied since April. A special lunch was laid on at the *Royal Hotel* which consisted of lobster, salmon mayonnaise, cutlets in aspic, supreme of chicken béchamel, forequarter of lamb, roulade veal, ox tongue, roast beef, asparagus, tipsy cake, Benedictine jelly, gooseberry tart, French pastry and dessert. This was followed by a special entertainment which included the famous actor, John Lawrence Toole, starring in the farce, *The Spitalfields Weaver*.

With the reorganisation of local government the following year, the Great Clacton Local Board was dissolved and in its place came the Great

Clacton Urban District Council, changed after six months to the Clacton Urban District Council (CUDC), which was to play a major part in the life of the town for the next 80 years. The first chairman was Henry Finer, a man who had the best of both worlds. Originally a shopkeeper in Great Clacton, he moved down into the new town to open up Clacton-on-Sea's first grocery shop in Rosemary Road.

The local authority, first as the Board and then as the CUDC, put its full weight behind attracting visitors to the town. In August 1893 the Local Board bought the greensward between Tower Road and Thoroughgood Road, gradually adding the greensward, cliffs and foreshore for the entire

34 *Most of the bathing machines on Clacton's beach belonged to Mr A. Cattermole, but some belonged to Messrs Almond and Maskell as seen here in this late Victorian photograph. Mr Almond is first on the left; Mr Maskell is third from the left.*

distance between Wash Lane in the west and Connaught Gardens in the east. They took the opportunity to fill in the old gaps that had been cut in the cliffs and laid out promenades and cliff walks. The cliffs themselves were landscaped and planted while seats, shelters and public conveniences were provided.

In 1913 the council bought Pier Gap together with the shops which then lined the road and embarked on what they termed a 'general beautifying programme', removing the shops and replacing them with landscaped gardens and a bridge to link the upper promenades. As part of the programme a new sunken amphitheatre incorporating the old bandstand was erected near the entrance to the pier with a glass-enclosed colonnade to the seaward side to protect it from the wind. At the opening ceremony for the whole enterprise the Mayor of West Ham congratulated the Council for carrying out the work by direct labour and for 'replacing the winkle and eel-pie shops previously down either side of the pier gap with beautiful flower beds and the bridge which stretched from cliff to cliff'.

Meanwhile the Land Company also continued to encourage visitors to Clacton. The pier was lengthened and services down the Thames run by the London Steamboat Co. and the General Steam Navigation Co. brought visitors in their thousands. Between 1880 and 1890 the number of passengers increased from 6,780 to 71,922, while the number

35   *Marine Parade West in the early years of the last century, c.1903. On the beach is the Yorkshire Pierrots concert party stand as well as several other kiosks. To the right centre of the photograph is the covered slope of the Reno Electric Stairway. This was an escalator which carried visitors up the cliff face for 1d. a time. It was erected in 1902, but in 1906 the company operating the escalator said they were losing money and asked the CUDC for permission to remove the structure. It was eventually removed in 1909 and a path put in its place.*

of promenades along the pier increased from 31,579 to 224,713.

After 1882 the railway too brought visitors in their thousands. And Clacton responded by opening more and more hotels and guest houses, more and more shops and restaurants, and laying on more and more amusements and entertainments. One of the largest of these facilities was Riggs' Retreat, opened in 1886 in Ellis Road. This could cater for between 1,200 and 1,300 visitors per day and it was estimated that in the first two weeks of July that year, out of an estimated 13,000 visitors to Clacton, Riggs catered for over 8,000 of them.

Even before the Operetta House, a new theatre, the Pavilion, had opened on the pier in 1893. In addition to these indoor theatres, open-air concert parties were beginning to sprout up all over the place. Probably the first of these was a group called L'Art Minstrels, who arrived in Clacton around 1892/3. They were followed by Jack Holland's

36 *(above) A photograph dating from c.1908 showing the new shelters and paths which had recently been laid out by the council along the cliff top in a bid to make the area more attractive to visitors.*

37 *(above right) A view of the West Promenade at high tide, c.1910. Part of the building on the right housed a sea water pumping station, built in 1900 to pump sea water to stand pipes dotted around the town from which council workmen could draw off water in order to clean the streets. Residents could buy a key so that they too could use the water to bathe their weary feet.*

38 *(right) The large postcard publishers did their bit to make Clacton an attractive holiday destination, as this comic card published c.1904 by Valentine's of Dundee shows.*

Esplanade and Beach, Clacton-on-Sea   I am simply "held" by the charms here

Concert Party, Braide and Partridge's White Minstrels, Ted O'Grady's Alfresco Entertainers, the Scarlet Mister E's, the Yorkshire Pierrots, the Jolly Coons, the White Coons and the troupe that was to have the longest lasting effect on Clacton of them all, Graham, Russell and Bentley's London Concert Company. The London Concert Company first arrived in 1894 and, after trying out several sites around the town, they eventually settled in a place called the West Cliff Gardens. At first they performed in the open air just like the rest, but eventually a timber frame theatre was built with canvas sides that could be raised during good weather and lowered when it rained. Russell died in 1910 and the company continued as Graham and Bentley's

39 *The programme for the formal opening of the new Band Pavilion, 27 May 1914. The proceedings opened with lunch at the Palace-by-the-Sea, with the main after dinner speaker being Mr H.K. Newton, the local MP. This was followed by the formal opening of the 'New Pier Approach Bridge' and the Band Pavilion by Colonel J. Humphrey, Alderman and Sheriff of the City of London. The whole ceremony was then brought to a close with a programme of music played by HM Royal Scots Greys.*

40 *The pier, c.1893. It looks as though work is in progress on lengthening the pier and has just started on building the Pavilion.*

41 *Clacton's bandstand was built in 1899 just to the east of the pier. This photograph was taken in 1904.*

42 *As part of the council's 'General Beautifying Programme', the bandstand was moved into the new Band Pavilion in 1914. This provided more seating and a wind shield. The view dates from that year.*

43   *Clacton's first railway station opened in 1882. This view dates from the early 1920s. The station was demolished following the erection of the new station in 1928.*

44   *Electric Parade, c.1904. The first shops in this street opened in 1901 with another tranche following in 1902. It was the first street in Clacton to be lit by electricity, hence the name. To the left of this photograph is Newson's outfitters, the only shop to have survived the hundred years since its opening. It is still owned and run by direct descendants of its founder, Ernest Newson.*

Concert Party. In 1912 they were joined by a young 'Romantic Baritone' called Stanley Holloway, who stayed with them until 1914. Graham and Bentley eventually went on to found the West Cliff Theatre.

In 1887, a Band Committee was formed and a band engaged, under the direction of George Badger, to play for 'seven hours at least per day'. The Bandstand was built in 1899. In 1906, the author and playwright, G.R. Sims, opened the Palace-by-the-Sea. This was an 'up-to-date' attraction modelled on the Earl's Court exhibitions then in vogue in Edwardian London. It contained yet another theatre for Clacton as well as large pleasure grounds in which were many attractions such as a

45 *Fred Pullan's Yorkshire Pierrots, c.1907. The Pierrots appeared on the West Beach near the pier every season from 1901 to 1912. In August 1912 an unusually high tide washed their stand out to sea and they decided not to risk it any more!*

46 *Harry Frewin's Jolly Coons in 1910. The Jolly Coons lasted longer than most concert parties in Clacton, returning after the First World War to appear on the Jetty.*

47 *A view taken from near the Jetty, c.1908, showing Harry Frewin's Jolly Coons' stand with a show in progress.*

band stand, Illuminated Electric Fountains, the Blue Caves of Capri, a Neapolitan Pergola, a Japanese Pagoda and the Madeira Promenade. The cinema formally arrived in 1911 with the conversion of the Operetta House into a cinema, although Messrs Russell and Bentley had introduced the cinematograph into London Concert Company shows as far back as 1898. In 1913 Clacton's first purpose-built cinema, the Kinema Hall, later the Kinema Grand, was opened in West Avenue.

The town was doing its best to provide the visitor with modern attractions and entertainments and this resulted in crowds flocking to the resort in the period before the First World War. To keep up with the demand, the town itself was expanding in all directions, both east and west along the sea front and back towards Great Clacton. The land being developed to the west had belonged to the Round Family and this was laid out for building on fields between the Palace and Wash Lane, at the foot of

which a small jetty was built in 1898 so that barges could unload building materials. Large hotels were being built, including the *Towers* in 1891 and the *Grand* in 1897, described by Pevsner as 'like a block of Kensington flats, red brick with many white ornamented friezes of foliage, putti, etc.' Other large hotels included the *Waverley* (originally built as a school) and the *Beaumont Hall*.

In 1904 Clacton-on-Sea came to the attention of the whole nation when the Government decided to test British readiness to invade a foreign country should the need arise. For the purposes of the exercise, Clacton was designated a foreign country and was defended by the 'Red Army' under Major General A.S. Wynne, which the British Expeditionary Force (the 'Blue Army') under General Sir John French was now attempting to invade. The Duke of Connaught was appointed umpire-in-chief of the proceedings. The manoeuvres had been well publicised beforehand and hundreds of sightseers

48 The London Concert Company in the grounds of the West Cliff Gardens in 1913. Second from the right is the company's founder, Bert Graham. Seated left is his partner, Will Bentley, while standing first left is the young romantic baritone who made such an impression that he was whisked away by Leslie Henson to star in London, Stanley Holloway.

49 The Palace-by-the-Sea, opened in 1906, was a large pleasure complex on Clacton's west cliff in 1906. In the background of this view taken c.1908 is one of Clacton's Martello towers.

Neapolitan Pergola, Palace by the Sea,
Clacton - on - Sea.

111086

lined Clacton's Marine Parade on the morning of 6 September 1904 to witness the invasion. In all about 150,000 troops came ashore, overwhelming the defence forces. By 9 September they had 'captured' Colchester and reached as far as Witham. At this point time and money ran out and the Blue Army retreated to Clacton, re-embarking at about 10.30 a.m. on 13 September.

The general opinion was that the manoeuvres had taught Britain nothing because they were hedged about with many absurd restrictions. For example, the invading forces had been told they must keep to the main roads as the Treasury had wanted to keep compensation payments for damage to crops down to a minimum. The famous author, Edgar Wallace, writing in the *Daily Mail*, dubbed Clacton the 'Capital of Letspretendia'. The country may have learned little but Clacton Council and local hoteliers and traders were delighted with the crowds and all the national publicity that the manoeuvres had attracted.

50 *(left)   One of the Palace's attractions, the Neapolitan Pergola, c.1906, just after the opening.*

51 *(below left)   After the Palace-by-the-Sea was closed shortly before the First World War, all that was left was its theatre. Starring in a play called* The Barber and the Cow *in the 1920s were Cedric Hardwick, John Gielgud and Laurence Olivier. This view is part of souvenir set issued in 1906 to mark the opening of the Palace.*

52 *(below)   The West Beach and Jetty, c.1904. The Jetty had been erected in 1898 for the use of barges bringing building materials to Clacton-on-Sea. It proved to be unsuccessful and was turned into a small pleasure pier between the wars. It was demolished in 1940 as a wartime precaution.*

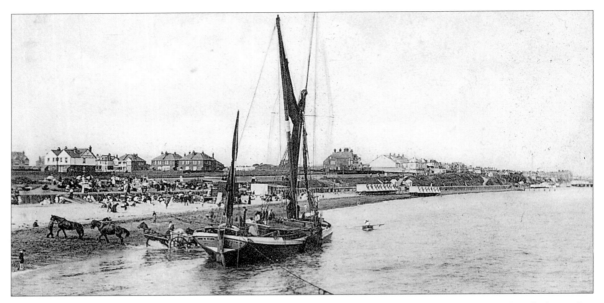

53   *This 1910 photograph shows why the Jetty was unsuccessful. Barges used to ignore it and run up onto the beach, unload, wait for high tide and float off again. The horses taking the material up the beach belonged to Zach Fairclough, a well-known local businessman.*

54   *This view of the Home Counties Brigade church service was taken c.1905, from King's Road at the west end of Clacton. The Annual Camp started in 1896 and continued until the First World War. Each summer hundreds of men, mostly territorials, would arrive for the annual training. Occasions such as the church service attracted large crowds of friends and relatives.*

55   *Part of the 150,000 contingent of troops landing on Clacton beach for the 1904 military manoeuvres, watched by a large crowd of holidaymakers.*

By 1914 Clacton was well on the way to becoming a major seaside resort after just 40 years of existence. But its progress and development came to a grinding halt as war was declared. Within one week of the announcement, the novelist, Arnold Bennett, reported that, 'The family went to Clacton this morning. They said it was practically emptied of visitors.' Some limited entertainments continued at the two cinemas and at the West Cliff Gardens Theatre but the trenches cut in the cliffs and the numerous pillboxes made it impossible to forget there was a war on, and to all intents and purposes Clacton's whole *raison d'être* as a seaside town was under threat.

VI

The Boom Years

WHEN the First World War finished Clacton returned to the business of packing in the visitors and providing them with entertainments. The council was once again in the forefront of this activity as one of its first actions was to fill in the cliff-top trenches and replace them with flower gardens, including the Garden of Remembrance.

But it was the arrival of one man and his family who were perhaps more responsible than anyone else for propelling Clacton–on–Sea to the very top of the seaside resort league in this country. Ernest Kingsman had established a holiday camp for ex-soldiers at Lowestoft in conjunction with the YMCA. His main problem was finding cheap transport from London. With trains and buses proving too dear, Kingsman turned his attention to paddle steamers. On investigating this possibility, it came to his attention that the Coast Development Corporation, a successor company to the old Clacton Land Co., which controlled the Belle Steamer fleet and the piers at Clacton, Walton, Southwold and Felixstowe, was in liquidation so he approached the liquidator with a view to re-establishing regular steamer services taking ex-soldiers to Lowestoft and anyone else who wanted to go to Clacton, Southwold and Lowestoft.

56 *An aerial view of Clacton, c. 1922, before Ernest Kingsman got to work on the pier. The town is still mainly centred on the area from Tower Road to Anglefield and back to Rosemary Road, but there is now development in all directions.*

The following year, 1921, Kingsman again met the liquidator with a view to renewing the contract, but this time the liquidator suggested that Mr Kingsman buy the company, all £350,000 worth, and see if he could make a go of it. In total, the company comprised five Belle Steamers, four piers, two hotels, a waterworks and other odds and ends of property around the east coast. Kingsman agreed and the deal was settled.

After discussing it with his wife, Ada, and son, Barney, Kingsman promptly sold everything except Clacton pier, which he considered had the best potential. Even though it was by this time fairly derelict, with just the Pavilion at one end and another small building at the entrance, both in a poor state of repair, Kingsman felt that Clacton was ideally situated to attract visitors from London. In his first season in charge, he rigged up a tarpaulin

57 One of Clacton's new gardens laid out in the early '20s after filling in the cliff top trenches.

58 The War Memorial in the Garden of Remembrance was unveiled on 6 April 1924 by the Rt Hon. Lord Lambourne, the Lord Lieutenant of Essex. It had first been proposed at a public meeting in the town in 1918, from which a committee of 90 was set up to oversee its erection. It was designed by Mr C.L. Hartwell ARA. This photograph dates from c.1930.

roof over some poles under which visitors danced to a band. It was not too secure and, on the many rainy nights that season, the dancers had to hold umbrellas over their heads while they danced. Much of his first year, however, was spent in making necessary repairs to the structure of the pier and he did not have time to think much about what he wanted to do with it.

Its success as an entertainments centre began in Kingsman's second season, 1922. This is how Kingsman described what happened in an interview he gave to *Tit Bits* magazine in 1934:

> At the beginning of my second season, while we were still busy with repairs, a young man

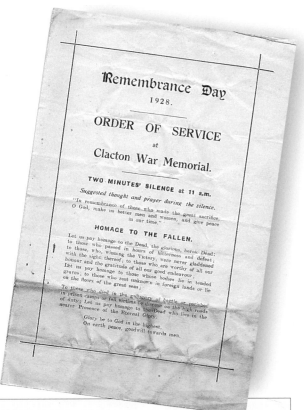

59 *Ever since the unveiling of the War Memorial, Clacton's Remembrance Day service has taken place in front of it. This is the programme for the 1928 service.*

60 *A view of the War Memorial with the pier in the background. Lined up on the Marine Parade are the horse-drawn hackney carriages which were a popular visitor attraction from the 19th century until the 1960s. One further licence was issued in 1981 but the attempted revival did not last long.*

wandered into my office and asked if he could give daily shows for the children. He said he had done a little concert party work and could make kiddies laugh. I sent him along to my foreman with instructions for a small open-air dais to be set up, with a carpet in front for the kiddies to sit upon. It was ready that same night. The next afternoon, I heard a hullabaloo and came out of my office to see the cause. At the end of the pier a thousand people were standing, and scores of children sitting on the bit of carpet, and they were shrieking with laughter, while the young man, aided by a couple of children from the audience, played a burlesque drama … It was a riot – and that was the beginning of Bertram …

It was also the beginning of Kingsman's £200,000 investment over the next 15 years. This money went on building three theatres, the Ocean Theatre, the Children's Theatre and the open-air Ramblas Concert Party Theatre; the Blue Lagoon Dance

Hall, which could accommodate something like 750 couples on the dance floor; the Crystal Casino Amusement Arcade; the first open-air pier swimming pool in the country; a zoo; a funfair; a restaurant; a home-made doughnut stand, which was said to take as much as £10 on a good day; a large roller coaster, the Steel Stella, and an extra berthing arm to allow four paddle steamers to dock at any one time, as well as enlarging the pier to make it the widest in the country. And the crowds flocked in, with anything up to 40,000 people in a single day passing through the turnstiles. The pier became known as no.1 North Sea and was undoubtedly a major factor in the rise of Clacton to the premier division of British seaside resorts during the 1920s and '30s.

At the other end of the town, the old jetty, which had never been particularly successful as an

61 *(left)* *A view of the pier in 1923 just after Ernest Kingsman had started work on converting it from a landing stage into an entertainment centre.*

62 *(below left)* *Clown Bertram, the man who convinced Ernest Kingsman that he was right to convert Clacton Pier into an entertainment centre. Bertram's open-air show was so popular with children and adults alike that Kingsman built him his own 500-seat theatre on the pier. But even this was not big enough to cater for the crowds that wanted to see him and he was eventually moved in to the 1,000-seat Pavilion which was renamed the Jollity Theatre.*

63 *(below)* *Sir John Pybus, local MP and Minister for Transport, opens the Pier Swimming Pool in 1932. He lived in the Old Moot Hall on Marine Parade East.*

64 (left) As well as being a popular venue for holidaymakers, the Pier Swimming Pool was also home to Clacton's water polo team.

65 (right) At one time there was a circus housed on the pier. This picture was taken on 23 August 1937.

66 (below) For Ernest Kingsman, new buildings and improvements never stopped. The construction on the left was to house the new dodgems track in the late 1930s.

67 *The West Clacton estate, c.1926, in the days before Butlin's arrived. It contained boating lakes and a miniature golf course.*

unloading place for barges, became a small pleasure pier in its own right, as part of the West Clacton Estate. As well as the amusement arcades and open-air shows operating on the jetty, the West Clacton Estate also boasted boating lakes and a miniature golf course.

The West Cliff Gardens Theatre was completely rebuilt in 1928 and opened as the West Cliff Theatre. The Princes Theatre was opened in 1931 as part of the new Town Hall complex, while in 1936 the old Bandstand was removed and replaced by a proper stage and auditorium. By 1939 four more cinemas had opened in Clacton: the Electric Theatre in Great Clacton in 1922; the Palace, converted from the Palace Theatre; and, in 1936, the Odeon and the Century, making six cinemas in all. Other attractions for visitors included Marshall's Amusements in Pier Avenue, opened in 1932; the regular weekly fête held at the John Groom Orphanage in Old Road; the opening of Vista Road Recreation Ground in 1929, which had the added attraction of

Essex playing county cricket there for one week during the season; and the Clacton Carnival begun by Ernest Kingsman in 1922 as a fund-raising event for Clacton Hospital.

When Butlin's arrived in 1937 it seemed as if Clacton had found its niche as one of the country's leading resorts. Most of its economy and employment depended on the holiday trade, which catered for 100,000 visitors per week during the summer who came not only to enjoy the entertainments but also the three miles of golden sand and the enviable sunshine record. For although Clacton was on the east coast, it had a south-facing prospect which meant that it gained a deserved reputation for long hours of warm sunshine, giving rise to the appellation 'Sunny Clacton'. The visitors were mostly from the East End of London or from the Midlands. The railway played a significant role in the continuing popularity of Clacton. As the paddle steamer trade declined, the railway proved to be of great significance as Clacton was able to cash in on

68 *The West Clacton estate included within its facilities the Jetty, seen in the background, and the Martello tower guarding Wash Lane, which was used as a café.*

69 *The West Beach and Jetty, c.1937. This view shows the Jetty in use between the wars as a small pleasure pier. To its right is Butlin's new Pleasure Park.*

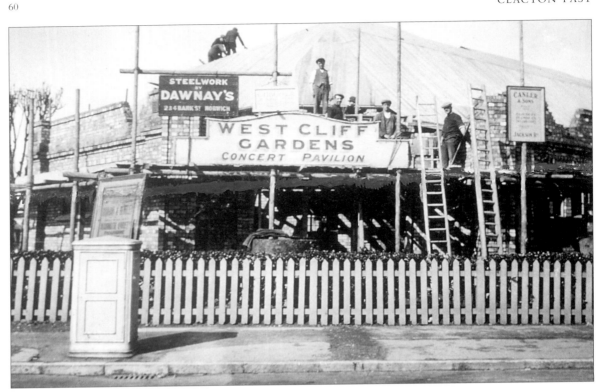

NEW BAND PAVILION, CLACTON-ON-SEA.

70 *(left)   The new West Cliff Theatre was built in 1928. It was designed by local architect Mr G.W. Gould and building was carried out by Canler and Sons of Jackson Road.*

71 *(below left)   The new Band Pavilion stage and auditorium were built in 1936, from which year this view dates. Many top dance bands played there both before and just after the Second World War.*

72 *(below)   A view of the West Beach in the 1930s, showing a couple of pleasure boats lined up to take trippers out. In the centre of the picture the striped Punch and Judy stand of Claude North can just be made out.*

both its proximity to London, little more than 1½ hours from Liverpool Street by train, and its direct line to Cambridge and the Midlands, with a regular Saturday service to Leicester and Birmingham.

The increasing number of visitors taking to the roads, whether in private cars or charabancs, was also well catered for, with the main A12 arterial road carrying visitors from the heart of London to within a few miles of Clacton. An even bigger boost was provided when the Colchester by-pass

The Bridge & Pier Approach
Clacton-on-Sea.

was opened in 1933, built almost exclusively to cope with Clacton's growing holiday trade. The town itself was always kept clean and the main tree-lined shopping streets had a light airy feel so that visitors could enjoy their trips round the big chain stores such as Woolworth's, Marks & Spencer and W.H. Smith, all of which arrived between the wars. There were also many well-known local shops such as Grimwade & Clarke, E.H. Newson & Sons, Gilders & Brown and Cook & Eaves. First-class restaurants abounded – Foyster's, the Geisha, Prince's and the Bohemian Café – while even more hotels, such as the *Oulton Hall*, were built along the sea-front.

Clacton was on top of the world and Clac-tonians were proud to be Clactonians. It was during the late '20s and early '30s that this pride was manifested in the building of three large public buildings. First, in 1928, was Clacton County High School. Second, in 1929, the new railway station.

73 *Pier Gap and Clacton's flag pole, c.1934. In the background the Pier Swimming Pool can be seen.*

74 *This view of the corner of Marine Parade and Pier Avenue, c.1924, has a summery feel about it and shows how popular Clacton was becoming as a sea-side resort during this period.*

75 *Between the wars Clacton became a very popular place to hold a procession! This one is shown making its way along Carnarvon Road opposite the railway station.*

TOWN HALL AND RAILWAY STATION FROM THE
CLACTON-ON-SEA.

76 *The corner of Pier Avenue and Rosemary Road, c.1925, in the days when Hayes Road cut across the corner and continued on to Pier Avenue; the road lay-out was redesigned in 1950.*

77 *An aerial view of Clacton from 1934 showing two of the proud town's new public buildings. To the bottom left is the Town Hall, while across the gardens to the north-east is the railway station.*

And finally, in 1931, HRH Prince Arthur of Connaught KG opened the new Town Hall in Station Road amidst due pomp and ceremony. The town of Clacton continued to expand at a rapid rate in all directions, and by the end of the '30s had even gone beyond the footprint of Great Clacton village with the building of Burrsville Park Estate, an estate built on the old Burrs Farm by Mr W. Renshaw. Begun in 1931, by 1936 it had grown into a small town in its own right consisting of 350 bungalows

along with a post office, draper, greengrocer, fishmonger, boot and shoe repairer, stationer, newsagent and confectioner and general provision store.

Just before the Second World War broke out Clacton had its own tragedy when a fire destroyed most of one side of the lower end of Pier Avenue, including the old Public Hall and a number of well-known shops. It started in the back yard of Lewellen's ironmongery store just before three o' clock on the afternoon of Sunday 4 June 1939 and was not brought under control until six o'clock. Hourly updates on the progress of the fire were broadcast on BBC Radio throughout the afternoon and the story made the front page of the next day's *Daily Mirror*. On the following morning large numbers of sightseers gathered to gaze upon the desolation never before seen in the town's history.

78 *The Lewellen's fire at its height on the afternoon of 4 June 1939. It was attended by fire crews from Clacton and Colchester. Butlin's also sent along its own fire tender to help out.*

What was once the most imposing block of shops in the town was now a mass of twisted girders and fallen masonry. Just two months later World War Two broke out and Clacton was never to be quite the same again. Perhaps the Lewellen's fire had been an omen ...?

79 *The scene of destruction in Pier Avenue the morning after.*

VII

Holland-on-Sea and Jaywick

AT EITHER END of Clacton-on-Sea are the two seaside resorts of Holland-on-Sea and Jaywick Sands, both now with large residential populations but with very different histories.

Holland-on-Sea

Holland-on-Sea as a name only dates from the first half of the 20th century and reflects its new status as a seaside resort. Its name since the Middle Ages had been Little Holland. The name Holland itself was first recorded *c*.1000 as Holande, Domesday Book referring to it as Holanda. The name means 'cultivated land by a hill-spur' and shows that, although on the sea, Little Holland was an agricultural rather than a maritime village. Having said that, however, the sea did play a big part in the contribution Little Holland was able to make to farming; the monks of St Osyth, to whom the land belonged in the Middle Ages, complained that it was 'rendered unprofitable by the frequent inundation of the sea'. Like most seaside villages on the Tendring peninsula, Little Holland suffered greatly from coastal erosion.

Maybe because of this Little Holland was never a large village, and in fact there is some record of it even declining over the centuries. In 1428 ten households were recorded, whereas by 1650 this had been reduced to eight. In this year it was agreed that its church benefice should be united with St John's at Great Clacton, the parish church being demolished some nine years later. Before its demise the church did manage to produce one incumbent of note in Thomas Evans, who was presented to the rectory in 1618 and held the benefice until his death in 1633. In his time he was well known as a poet. The old parish church was situated close to Little Holland Hall, the residence occupied by successive lords of the manor, though even this fell into disuse and by the 18th century was reduced to nothing more than a farmhouse.

Further east along the coast, Holland Brook ran out into the sea at the estuary know as the Gunfleet. The name Gunfleet has long since been transferred to the sandbank some four miles off the shore and the estuary itself worn away by constant erosion.

As well as the problems with coastal erosion, Little Holland also suffered by being mainly cut off from other villages in the area, only one road entering the village from Colchester and terminating at the gates of the Hall. In the second half of the 18th century another road was built continuing out of Little Holland to Great Holland and on to Kirby and Walton. But, in spite of this, the village remained a tiny, sleepy hamlet.

All this was to change at the end of the 18th century when Little Holland, along with Great Clacton, saw the start of much activity associated with the threat posed by the expected Napoleonic invasion. In 1795 a signal station was built on the cliffs and from then, until the threat of invasion subsided some 20 years later, the whole area became

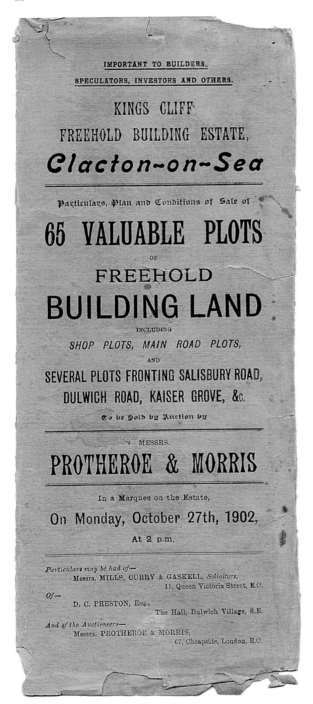

one of intense military activity with large military encampments being established on the cliffs. This led to the arrival of something like 3,000 troops in the Little Holland area amongst a resident population of just under sixty.

As part of the military build up a gap was cut in the cliffs to provide access to the beach. Originally known as Shore Lane, the track from the beach up to the main Colchester Road eventually became known as York Road. A Martello tower was erected in 1809, but unlike the Clacton towers it is no longer in existence. In fact, it only lasted for about ten years before it was demolished.

Oddly enough, while all this was going on there were the first indications that one day Little Holland might become a seaside resort, as in 1799 a Mr John Harrison of Great Bromley Hall recorded that 'Some of the Servants being ill of a fever I removed the Nurses and Children to the Old Manor House of Little Holland Hall … beautifully situated close to the sea on the Essex Coast where they remained for six weeks.' In 1811 a farm was offering 'every facility for sea bathing'. But, for the most part, agriculture continued to be the mainstay of the village. There were four main farms in the village, the Hall Farm, Bushell's Farm (later Bennett's Farm), Brickhouse Farm and Ransome's Farm (later to become the *Oakwood Inn*). As well as the farms, the village had one small beer house, the site of which was eventually to become the *Roaring Donkey*, and five farm cottages. For much of the 19th century these ten buildings constituted the whole of Little Holland.

Life was still hard for local farmers and farmworkers through the century and they were not helped by a major agricultural depression in the 1890s. By this time the neighbouring villages of Clacton and Frinton had both begun to look into the possibility of redefining themselves as seaside resorts rather than rely on agriculture for a living. In both cases it was the energy and foresight of one

80 *The early days of the last century were marked by many sales of land in Holland. This one took place on 27 October 1902 and was for 65 plots of land on the Kings Cliff Estate.*

81 *Before building really took off in Holland, many families came to the area to spend their holidays in the many bell tents that dotted the area. This is the Stewart family from London camping in an area around what is now Lyndhurst Road in the early years of the last century.*

man that had begun to transform the villages. In Clacton, as we have seen, it was Peter Bruff, while in Frinton it was a man called Richard Powell Cooper, who had started to adapt a village even smaller than Little Holland. In Little Holland the part of the seaside resort entrepreneur was played by David Cripps Preston, who was to change completely the ancient village of Little Holland and turn it in to the seaside resort of Holland-on-Sea.

Preston was born in Bedford in 1843 and had moved to Dulwich Village near London where he began to develop building estates. On 27 June 1900 most of the land comprising the village of Little Holland came up for sale by auction, the only exception being the land owned by Ransome's Farm (by then Kent's Farm). Preston bought the lot with the sole intention, like Bruff and Powell, of turning it into a seaside resort. His first act was to divide the land up into four separate building estates known as King's Cliff, Queen's Cliff, Empire and Preston Park. King's Cliff (named for the forthcoming

coronation of Edward VII) was the first to be developed and the estate was divided into individual plots with provisions for shops, an inn and a hotel.

It wasn't all plain sailing for Preston, however, and his plans were frustrated when he put forward an application to the licensing authority for a provisional licence to enable the proposed hotel to sell intoxicating liquor. Preston considered the hotel crucial to his plans to develop the resort as he saw it as a place in the first instance for those buying the other individual plots to have a place to meet contractors, surveyors and others and conduct their business, and as somewhere to stay while they supervised the building of their individual plots. Secondly, in the longer term, he saw it as a vital element in attracting holidaymakers to the resort. Greene King, however, as the owners of the beer house, by now called the *Princess Helena*, objected as they saw it as a threat to their business. The licensing authority upheld Greene King's objections and refused to grant Preston a licence.

82 *At the top of the cliff is the* King's Cliff Hotel, *which eventually opened in 1932 when the seaside resort began to take off. Many of the facilities on the beach were supplied by local builder Walter Johnston. One of his beach huts, decorated in his identifying orange and white stripes, stands in splendid isolation before work really started.*

Because of this setback building almost came to a complete standstill. Two houses were built in 1902, a third was added in 1903, while between 1904 and 1908 just seven further houses were built. In 1903 a corrugated iron church was opened on land donated by Preston and in 1905 the first shop was opened on the corner of Frinton Road and King's Avenue. With the shop, the church and two of the houses being built near the *Princess Helena*, it was, ironically, around this area that the nucleus of Holland-on-Sea began to grow, while Preston's favoured centre near his proposed hotel at the other end of King's Avenue, on the junction with King's Parade, failed to develop. By the outbreak of the First World War the population had risen from 92 in 1901 to just one hundred and forty.

With the coming of war Holland was once again to become the centre of military activity as trenches were dug on the cliff top and soldiers returned to patrol the seafront cliffs.

With the war over and people looking to enjoy themselves, building at last took off in Holland and the 1920s saw a big growth in the population. As early as 1921 the population had almost doubled to 247 and Preston, by now in his 80s and in failing health, once again put forward an application for a licence for his proposed hotel, but once again it was turned down. David Cripps Preston died in 1925, knowing that at last his resort of Holland-on-Sea had begun to take off but still bitterly disappointed not to have seen his hotel get off the ground. With the growth in population there were many calls for better services. In the early '20s

83 The Roaring Donkey, *built on the site of the* Princes Helena, *formerly the Beer House. The owners, Greene King, prevented David Preston from obtaining a licence for his planned hotel for many years as they felt it would adversely affect their trade.*

there was still no electricity, gas, mains water, sewerage or refuse collection. At that time Little Holland was included in the Tendring Rural District and had no direct representation on the council as it was included within the Great Holland ward. Consequently, in 1923, a public meeting was called to demand parish council status and to petition Essex County Council to that effect. The County Council's reply was swift, and within two weeks Little Holland had its own parish council with Major Walter Williams of Oakwood Hall elected the first chairman. The council continued the fight for basic services as the population continued to rise. By the time of the 1931 census it had reached 780.

Eventually Preston's long-hoped-for hotel opened for business in 1932, having been given its licence in 1927. It was a final irony in this drawn-out affair that shortly before completion the hotel, the *King's Cliff*, was purchased by Greene King. With little progress to show for all its efforts, the Parish Council was put under further pressure by a number of local action groups which sprang up. One, the Holland Ratepayers Association, took it on themselves to contact Clacton Urban District Council to see if they would be interested in an amalgamation. Tendring Rural District Council was not averse to such a suggestion as they felt they did not have the financial wherewithal to support the growth of Little Holland and provide the services needed. Eventually, after discussions involving the three councils as well as Essex County Council, it was agreed to transfer Little Holland parish into Clacton Urban District Council under the name

84   *The Queen's Café, c.1934. Mr Johnston was also responsible for building the Queen's Café near the bottom of King's Avenue. As well as a café, the complex included shops and tea gardens to the rear.*

of Holland-on-Sea. The final meeting of the Parish Council was held on 31 March 1934 and the transfer took effect from the next day.

This was the last time the name Little Holland was used to describe the area, although it was not the first time Holland-on-Sea had been used. There is evidence that the name was first used as far back as 1904 and the Parish Council itself suggested a formal name change to Essex County Council in 1926. In 1927 the Post Office announced it would now be using the name Holland-on-Sea as the new town's postal address. By 1934, in fact, the only use of Little Holland was in the title of the Parish Council, but this disappeared with the council.

With all the developments going on in the village, it was necessary to improve the facilities available on and near the beach if visitors were to find it worth their while holidaying at Holland. Probably the first entertainment to be laid on was

by the Merry Maids, who gave performances of 'Song, Dance, Mirth and Melody' in a marquee on Frinton Road in 1929 and later on a patch of ground at the junction of King's Avenue and Madeira Road. But it was local builder and landowner, Walter Johnston, who really turned the place into a small seaside resort. Beginning in 1929, he built five wooden pavilions on the beach. The pavilions provided refreshments and cubicles to enable holidaymakers to change for bathing. He also built a number of beach huts for hire and there were organised games on the beach, the sandcastle competition proving very popular. In 1931 Johnston built a Public Hall and café at the King's Parade end of King's Avenue. In 1935 this was extended to become the Queen's Hall Theatre with nightly variety shows performed during the season.

Other facilities to be laid on during the 1930s included the Ainsworth Café in York Road, run by Mr and Mrs A. Kennell, tennis courts in Hereford

85 *In 1935 Mr Johnston extended the complex even further and built a theatre, the Queen's Hall. Summer shows were performed from 1935 to 1957. In 1958 the Holland Players, seen here, put on a short repertory season. The theatre was eventually demolished in 1972 and a block of flats built in its place.*

86 *Teddy Edwards, Hilda and their daughter Joan provided the entertainment for Holland's VE Day party in May 1945. This is Teddy Edwards – the one on the right! – c.1950.*

Road opened by Mr C.W. Cooke and Sunnick's Corner Shop in Primrose Road which provided refreshments. Much of the land belonging to the old Bennett's Farm in York Road that had not yet been built on was used for camping in the 1930s. The local newspaper reported in 1936 that Holland-on-Sea was 'literally covered with canvas'.

When the Second World War came many of the residents left the coastal defence strip area and entertainments were put on hold for the duration. Troops were moved into the area again and defences strengthened along the cliffs. Restrictions were eventually lifted in August 1944 (although the use of binoculars was still forbidden), and in May 1945 Holland-on-Sea celebrated VE Day with a party at the Public Hall, the entertainment laid on by Teddy Edwards, Hilda and Joan. Normality returned slowly after the war. The *King's Cliff Hotel* re-opened in 1946 and the Queen's Hall Theatre in 1949. New attractions sprang up, including the York Road

Bowling Green in 1949, and road and house building continued apace.

   In line with most British seaside resorts, including Clacton, Holland-on-Sea enjoyed a successful
era in the early '50s, but by the late '50s its fortunes
were beginning to decline a little as holidaymakers
began to look further afield. The Queen's Hall
Theatre closed and the emphasis began to shift
away from a holiday resort into a residential and
retirement area. And that is largely how it has
remained to this day. Expansion has continued but
there is now very little in the way of facilities for
holidaymakers (the last of Mr Johnston's pavilions
was demolished in the early '80s), although the
lower promenade is lined with beach huts and the
beach still attracts a fair number of visitors looking
for a quiet day out away from the brash lights and
amusement arcades of nearby Clacton.

Jaywick Sands

The name Jaywick was first recorded as Clakyn-
geywyk in 1438, meaning a dwelling or (dairy)
farm at the place associated with a man called Clacc
(in other words, Clacton's dairy farm). The Clacc
part was dropped in the 16th century and the name
contracted to Gey wyck (recorded in 1584). It
subsequently became standardised as Jewick and then
Jaywick. And a farm it remained until 1928, in
which year an entrepreneur in the tradition of Bruff
and Preston called Frank Christoffer Stedman
bought the land. Stedman already had a reputation
for building and developing housing estates, and by
the time he bought Jaywick had already been
responsible for estates at Sevenoaks, Rickmansworth,
Hastings, Horley, Bognor and Bexley.

   As soon as he bought the several hundred acres
that comprised Jaywick's farmlands and the

87 *Although not as brash as Clacton, Holland nevertheless became a popular place for family holidays, with the lower promenade lined
with beach huts, which is how it remains to this day.*

surrounding marshlands he set about developing them for housing. His first act was to open a property development office in Clacton and install his son Jack as resident manager. His next move was to build a road linking his proposed new estate with Clacton. Then came the serious business of building houses. But Stedman had not foreseen the trouble he would have over drainage, sewerage and flooding, which was a surprising oversight from a man of Stedman's experience given that Jaywick was on low-lying marsh land which reached right to the coast. However, in the spring of 1929 he built his first six houses, and by the summer had completed Golf Green Road and Beach Road (now The Broadway). It was at this point that he received his first warning about the problem of flooding from Clacton Urban District Council. But Stedman refused to believe them and in some notes he made at the time of his meeting with the council he said he believed the danger was remote. CUDC was reluctant to sanction the work Stedman wished to put in hand with the sewers, so that by the autumn of 1929 he was forced to stop building houses and instead submitted plans for beach huts.

In 1930 the council passed the plans for beach huts on condition they were not used for overnight accommodation. In his original advertisement, in the *Clacton Times* of 18 May 1929, Stedman had announced that roads and tree-lined avenues would give the estate a

> rural and peaceful atmosphere and the extension of Gas, Water, Electric Light etc. to be arranged. The Estate will put in Main Drainage. Well-known aviators would provide flights at Whitsun and a mile-long sporting lake of size and character such as is non-existent in any Seaside Resort in Great Britain is now in course of construction and would provide motor boat racing, water polo, aqua-planing and water carnivals.

Unfortunately for Frank Stedman, things were not working out quite as planned. At this point it looked as though his original grandiose idea of building a

88 *This was the sort of property that Mr Stedman was selling in the Brooklands and Grasslands areas of Jaywick. This advertisement dates from 1933.*

well-appointed housing estate by the sea had been reduced to beach huts for day visitors only and even the aviators were prosecuted for unlicensed flying! Only one part of Stedman's original plans came to fruition. In an area to the west of his proposed main estates he planned a 'fine beach for bathing houses' which could 'be built for £25'. This was the area which subsequently became Brooklands and Grasslands. In August 1929 the *Daily Chronicle* reported that 1,000 square feet of land with a hut was selling for £50 in Jaywick.

It was not all doom and gloom, however, as the beach houses sold well and within two years the number of freeholders had grown so large that the Jaywick Sands Freeholders Association was formed and held its first meeting on the Sunday before the

89   *A typical Brooklands road in the 1930s. All the roads were named after makes of popular car. This road is Bentley Avenue.*

1931 August Bank Holiday in the Jaywick Beach Café. Over 200 people turned up, the main gripe of the meeting being that the Post Office was not delivering letters to the individual houses but to pigeon holes outside the estate office.

Later on in 1931 Frank Stedman and representatives of the Freeholders Association pressed Clacton Council to lay on electricity. Again the question of possible flooding and drainage was raised by the councillors, who objected to Jaywick being connected to the electricity supply. The council once again raised the whole question of whether people should be sleeping in the huts at Jaywick.

To try to resolve the issue a public meeting was held on Easter Monday 1932, organised by the Jaywick Sands Freeholders Association. The meeting was attended by Stedman and by several Clacton councillors. Councillor Fenton-Jones put the council's position which was, basically, that they had made it clear all along to Mr Stedman that planning

permission had been granted on the clear understanding that the huts were to be used as beach huts only and not as domestic dwellings, and if Mr Stedman had allowed residents to think otherwise he had misled them. Stedman denied this and said the council had been perfectly aware all along that the huts were being slept in and had even sent a Medical Officer down who had made certain recommendations to render them suitable for sleeping and that these recommendations had been carried out.

The council agreed that because the freeholders had been misled, and because they realised many of them would suffer hardship if they kept strictly to the terms of their planning permission, they were willing to agree that if those huts already erected were to apply for a licence for a temporary building they would grant one for a period of three years, and renew it, provided certain improvements were carried out. The meeting rejected the proposal.

90 *An early warning for Jaywick. This flood occurred in 1936. The photograph shows Hillman Avenue, Brooklands.*

91 *Another view of the 1936 flood, this time showing Swift Avenue from the sea wall.*

OYEZ! OYEZ! OYEZ!

Whereas at JAYWICK in the parish of Clacton in the Tendering Hundred there is forthwith to be erected near the sea shore a TUDOR VILLAGE with houses for both rich and poore with swards and pleasaunces and a stockes for ye correction of malefactors and all things conformable do all ye GOOD CITIZENS hereby take notice that in ye said estate of Jaywick there be sundrie PLOTTES of goode high land now for sale at £65 with ye freeholde and for the better understanding of this matter ye are now to enquire of our RESIDENT AGENT AT JAYWICK SANDS ESTATE NEAR CLACTON·ON·SEA

92 One of Frank Stedman's adverts for his more upmarket estate, the Tudor Village, in 1936. The price for a three-bedroom semi-detached house in Tudor Green could be as much as £725.

93 This photograph taken in 1935 shows just how popular Jaywick Sands had become at that time, with hundreds of holidaymakers enjoying a day out on the beach.

94   *Another view of Jaywick beach in 1935.*

95   *This comic postcard from the 1930s reminded everyone that in spite of its continual battle with the CUDC, Jaywick still found time to become a popular seaside resort.*

During the following year negotiations continued, and at their 1932 AGM the Freeholders' Association was able to report that 'the difficulties had to a large extent been overcome' and a drainage scheme had been agreed. The scheme was to cost each hut £12 10s. and it was to be obligatory for all owners to connect to the sewers and water supply once they were laid on.

By this time, Stedman noted, the summer-time population of Jaywick was reaching 5,000. He and his son continued to advertise the site through every possible means. Beach hut and plot were still going for as little as £50 upwards freehold, and chalets were displayed at the Ideal Home Exhibition and at the Model Houses Exhibition. The Brooklands part of the estate, which had all its roads named after popular makes of motor car, was advertised as the 'Motorists Mecca by the Sea'. In the summer of 1934 Stedman presented a freehold bungalow

96   *Beach Road in the 1930s. On the right is the Café Morocco, a popular nightspot with dance hall before the war. After several changes of use it eventually closed down in 1987 and was demolished in 1991.*

for the benefit of the Essex Fund for the Blind. At a special fair held for the occasion, the leader of the Labour Party, George Lansbury, performed the handing-over ceremony. However, 1934 also saw the first serious flooding, when the sea came right over the wall and considerable damage was done to the Brooklands Estate. Mr Stedman paid for improved sea defences along the whole of the Brooklands front. In January and December 1936 there were more severe floods and the sea defences were further strengthened.

By now the Stedman family was promoting a new development of permanent houses a little further inland called the Tudor Village. And although Stedman experienced no problems with this development, Clacton Council once again turned its attention to his original development. Under a new town planning scheme, the council scheduled the original part of Jaywick, known as the Old Section (or Old Town), Brooklands and Grasslands as areas where permanent buildings would not be

permitted, the reason this time being that parts were too densely built upon, the land was not suitable and the cost of drainage and roadmaking would prove too onerous. The council required a density of ten dwellings per acre before it would consider approval for permanent building. Actual densities at the time were 29 to the acre in Brooklands and 20 in the Old Section. The Tudor Village had a density of nine to the acre.

At the time Jaywick residents were being refused planning permission to sleep in their houses Clacton Council was approving the Butlin's Holiday Camp just down the road. In fact, the proposals from Butlin's ran contrary to the new planning scheme just as much as Jaywick's did and were just as much a contravention of building by-laws. In spite of all its difficulties and continual battles with the council, Jaywick Sands had throughout the '30s become a popular holiday resort. The estate grew larger and larger, many shops were built and the whole place took on a sort of informal holiday camp atmosphere.

97 *Jaywick's miniature railway at Crossways station in 1936.*

For Londoners, in particular, it was very popular indeed.

An interesting development of the inter-war years was the Jaywick Miniature Railway, another Stedman idea, which opened on 31 July 1936. It ran from Jaywick Sands station along the old sea wall, down an embankment, through a tunnel, across marshlands and a stream, before reaching its terminus at Crossways Station. The fare for the return journey was 6d. for adults and 4d. for children. It ran every half-hour starting at 8.30 a.m. At its height it carried 2,000 passengers per day. It came to an end at the outbreak of the Second World War, when part of the land it ran over was needed for coastal defences and the track was lifted and used for scrap.

During the war Jaywick became a restricted area but it did receive some important visitors from the Ministry of Town and Country Planning. Their survey of the East Anglian coast from Hunstanton in Norfolk to Tilbury in Essex provided the basis for much of the post-war planning legislation. One

of the members of the Ministry team recorded his impressions of Jaywick:

> I found this extraordinary piece of holiday shack development surprising and rather interesting in a way, though it does leave one perhaps with a feeling of some nausea about it. There are many hundreds of wooden shacks erected without proper regard for the right use of materials or proper layout but it is an inescapable fact that the colony does provide for many thousands of holidaymakers each year to enjoy a holiday by the sea.

In the late 1940s sea protection work took on a degree of urgency because of the neglect suffered during the war. Once again the difference between how Clacton treated Jaywick and Butlin's was highlighted. The protection of Butlin's Holiday Camp was estimated to cost £50,000 and was carried out entirely at the expense of the local authority. That at Jaywick cost £30,000, of which £10,000 had to be contributed by the Jaywick Sands Freeholders' Association.

98 *Even before the 1953 floods, there were many attempts at shoring up the sea defences. One such, which took place in early 1950, was known as Adrian's Wall, after the Chairman of the Jaywick Freeholders Association, Adrian Wolfe, who continually agitated for such defences.*

The sea defences continued to exercise the minds of Jaywick residents. There were breaches of the sea wall in 1948, and in 1949 there was serious flooding in the Brooklands area. At the 1950 meeting of the Freeholders Association there was criticism of the committee for not doing enough and a new body, the Jaywick Ratepayers Association, was formed. This new organisation passed a resolution calling on Clacton Council to take over the 'town-planned section of Jaywick' and to adopt the roads. Councillor Quick pointed out that the mere adoption of a resolution, even assuming it was accepted by Clacton Council, 'would not convert Jaywick into a garden city overnight'. The residents of Jaywick became increasingly divided between the old Freeholders Association, which represented the people in the dwellings not officially recognised as permanent, and the Ratepayers Association, which mainly represented those on the Tudor Estate. Both groups, however, were still concerned with improving the sea defences and who was going to pay for it.

Unfortunately, the arguments were still going on when Clacton Council's worst fears were realised and the great tide struck Jaywick on the night of 31 January/1 February 1953. This was the result of a storm that had begun to the west of Scotland and worked its way round the north of Scotland and then down the east coast of England. By about midnight water was pouring over the sea wall at

Jaywick. The police were doing their best to warn the residents but, of course, this was no easy matter as it was never clear which of the houses had residents and which didn't. There were something like 1800 supposed seaside dwellings but, in fact, about 250 of them were being used as permanent homes.

At first the sea, driven by gale force winds, smashed through those chalets nearest the sea front, but a worse disaster was in store for Jaywick. The water had also breached the sea wall at St Osyth, sweeping in a torrent across the low-lying marshes

and battering Jaywick from the rear. It cut the town off completely, making rescue all but impossible. Only two people were able to get through, a Jaywick boatman and a police sergeant. Both worked throughout the night ferrying people to the one dry little island that remained in Jaywick, which, by a great stroke of luck, happened to be around the local Red Cross commander's flat in Beach Road. Most people were in bed when the disaster struck and had no time to escape. In all, 35 people died that night. Many others were injured or suffered from exhaustion and shock. They were taken to

Clacton Hospital as soon as the floods subsided enough for ambulances to get through, though this was not until many hours later. Others were taken to special rest centres set up in hotels such as the *Royal* and the *Oulton Hall* in Clacton.

Emergency repairs were carried out to the sea wall as soon as possible and the Essex River Board proposed a £100,000 scheme to raise the sea wall from Jaywick to Point Clear by two to three feet. By 1955, however, the Freeholders Association was still complaining that the sea defences were inadequate and the chairman, Mr Wolfe, pointed

99   *The real thing. The aftermath of the tragic 1953 floods.*

100   *The Broadway, looking east from Glebe Way in 1956, showing that Jaywick was still a busy place in the 1950s.*

out that £250,000 was being spent on a new sea defence scheme at Holland-on-Sea. Throughout the 1950s and '60s the same issues exercised the minds of Jaywick residents, though there was an even bigger influx of people coming to live here, mostly in retirement, and putting up better quality bungalows in the Old Town area.

By 1970, as the Old Town began to take on the air of a more permanent housing development, the Brooklands and Grasslands areas remained much the same as they always had, and in January 1971 Clacton Council decided it was about time they solved the problem once and for all. They put a compulsory purchase order on both sections with a view to clearing the area completely 'on the grounds that the whole estate was dilapidated and insanitary'. Some 90 chalet owners accepted the council's offer of £150 and their chalets were demolished. The Freeholders Association, however, would have none of it and they briefed a London

barrister to represent them at the subsequent public inquiry. The chairman of the inquiry, a representative of the Department of Environment, concluded that the residents of Brooklands and Grasslands should not be pushed around by the council just because their living conditions appeared to be sub-standard. In fact, he criticised the council for not laying on a proper water supply and drainage system. Rather than clearing the area, he concluded that Clacton Council had a duty to upgrade it.

Under the local government reorganisation of 1974, Tendring District Council took over responsibility for the area. However, and more importantly for the residents of Jaywick, the Anglian Water Authority took over responsibility for the drainage and finally, in 1980, they actually began to provide the sewers that the Freeholders Association had been agitating for since 1931. In 1975 Tendring District Council tried to compromise on the issue of planning permission for chalets in Brooklands

101 *Jaywick's bus terminus in 1956, showing the terminus of Eastern National's seafront service which ran from Jaywick to Clacton.*

and Grasslands. As long as certain minimum requirements were met, they were prepared to allow summer-time residence from 1 March to 31 October. The Residents Association rejected this on the grounds that the local authority had *de facto* accepted the permanent residency position for 40 years as they had charged the full rates.

The recent history of Jaywick has seen a continuation of the attempts to upgrade the facilities, most notably the roads and sea defences. In the late 1990s Jaywick was the subject of a successful £1,000,000 regeneration bid by Tendring Council and this money is going towards the upgrading of all facilities. As a seaside and holiday town, Jaywick has followed the fortunes of Clacton itself, popular in the '30s, late '40s and '50s, but declining from the '60s. Many of the residents now living in Jaywick are retired Londoners who have come to spend their twilight years by the sea.

VIII

Butlin's

IN MANY WAYS the story of Butlin's holiday camp, built at the western end of the town in the late 1930s, mirrors the story of Clacton itself. Both town and camp were born in years when important holiday legislation was being introduced in parliament. When first proposed, Butlin's attracted fierce opposition from one section of the resident population, while at the same time presenting opportunities to those members of the business community prepared to take them. It brought thousands of visitors to Clacton and attracted star names to its theatres and dance halls. Butlin's prospered in the pre-war and early post-war years, declined through the '60s and '70s and finally, unlike Clacton itself, totally collapsed, closing its doors in the 1980s and bringing to an end the tradition of weekly and fortnightly holidays in Clacton.

The first indication that Billy Butlin was interested in building a holiday camp in Clacton came when it was discovered he was a member of a

102   *Before Butlin's arrived, this was the nearest Clacton got to a holiday camp. The Jetty Camp was actually sited on the spot Butlin's would later occupy. This view dates from the Edwardian period.*

87

The Dining Hall, Butlin's Holiday Camp, Clacton-on-Sea. "Empire View". 25.

103   *A very early photograph of the camp shows the dining hall on 26 June 1938 just two weeks after the camp opened.*

business consortium which had bought the West Clacton Estate in 1936. This estate, originally developed by Frederick Wagstaff, Henry Foyster, George Gardiner and Robert Coan, had for a number of years been operating at the western end of Clacton's Marine Parade as a leisure area providing two boating lakes, four miniature golf courses, a small pier with amusements (the Jetty), and other activities 'where the visitor can find healthy recreation'.

Butlin already owned a string of pleasure parks around the English coastline from Mablethorpe in the north to Portsmouth in the south, as well as one on the Isle of Man. In 1936 he opened his first 'luxury holiday camp' at Skegness. It was an immediate success and Butlin, never slow to follow up a money-making idea, looked around for a suitable site for a second camp. He found one when the West Clacton Estate came on to the market in the middle of 1936. He very soon bought out his

consortium partners and in the autumn of that year he presented Clacton Council with the plans for his second holiday camp under the terms of the Town and Country Planning (General Interim Development) Order, 1933.

The sale of the West Clacton Estate had already been the cause of much controversy in the town, as one group of councillors, backed by the *Clacton Times*, had urged that the council itself purchase the land in order to provide a park and open space for residents and visitors alike to enjoy in perpetuity. The council, however, declined to take up this invitation and at the full council meeting held on 3 December 1936 they were called upon to consider Butlin's application.

The controversy in the town was reflected in the columns of the *Clacton Graphic* and the *Clacton Times*. The president of the Hotel & Boarding House Association, Mr. W. Adams, wrote a long letter savagely attacking the plans. He prefaced his letter

The Private Beach.
Butlin's Holiday Camp, Clacton·on·Sea.   "Empire View" 033-27.

104   *A scarce view of Butlin's private beach at the back of the camp in 1939, showing the Martello tower with the Jetty in the background.*

by denying that his opposition was in any way due to 'fear or jealousy … we have always welcomed all fair and reasonable competition'. He then went on to outline what, according to him, were his association's real objections:

> We have asked many residents whether they would be prepared to build good class property in the district in view of the proposal and in every case the answer has been 'No' … If the proposed structure were to be a good class hotel it would have our full support, as in spite of any alleged competition, it would, we feel tend to raise the tone of Clacton instead of lowering it …

His objections were countered, however, by a letter from Mr H.C. Dove of the *Warwick Castle Hotel*, who said that he had visited Skegness and had discovered that both shopkeepers and residents welcomed the Butlin's camp. 'Their business … had increased considerably. The boarding and private houses also find that the younger folk use the camp

and their older friends patronise them … Mr. Butlin's publicity will draw not only his own clients, but also many visitors to the town.' A Mr W. Dearsley added a new dimension when he wrote, 'I have a wife and family to support and I have been on the dole … I hope I shall be one of the 260 employees during the season.'

When the council finally met on 3 December the battle lines were drawn and the town was split in two over the application. Indeed the very first contribution to the debate by Councillor Fenton-Jones summed up the split very clearly as, although he was chairman of the Plans Committee, which was recommending acceptance of the application, he personally was opposed. Councillor Elliott summed up the opposition's main argument when he asked his fellow councillors if they could imagine people 'building decent houses at the back [of the camp]? Mr. Butlin's proposal would do away with the rights of people who had been paying high rates …'. Supporters of the application felt that, despite their protestations, the real reason behind the opponents' arguments was the effect on the small boarding houses. Councillor Laurie King dismissed this argument by saying, 'How could the camp affect the boarding houses? In the summer the town has a population of 100,000. The camp would cater for 1,500. That was 1½% of the total.' A number of different reasons were put forward in support of the camp – 'It means employment for hundreds of people', 'Clacton would benefit from Butlin's advertising', 'Butlin was planning to spend £7,000.'

But it was left to leading Labour Party councillor, Jack Shingfield, to put the whole debate into the context of its times with a powerful appeal for Clacton not to be left behind.

> The modern development is that people are going for their holidays in groups. It is the factory psychology. People live in towns and work in factories and are used to noise. They take the same sort of system in their holidays as they have in their ordinary everyday lives and that is the reason why these camps and group holidays are proving so successful.

He followed this up by referring to the 'Holidays with Pay' movement then gathering momentum throughout the country, and ended his plea by saying that, 'If a town is going to be successful it has to fit itself in with the demands made by the people of the country.' When the vote was taken, the supporters of the holiday camp won by 13 votes to six. This effectively silenced the opposition, although one last ditch attempt to scupper the proposals was made at an inquiry into the proposals of the Regional Town Planning Committee as they affected Clacton which was held at the Town Hall on 7 July 1937. This inquiry was called to deal mainly with Jaywick, but opponents of Butlin's were hoping to use it to set aside the council's decision. However, the inspector told those in attendance that he was not concerned with the West Clacton Estate or Butlin's and that the matter could not be raised at the inquiry.

As soon as the council reached its decision, Billy Butlin went into action. He began to clear the site and started work on a new pleasure park. The building of the holiday camp itself was delayed but Butlin decided to go ahead and open the park to visitors for the 1937 season. Conscious of the controversy his proposals had aroused, Butlin did his best to involve local people in his new enterprise. Consequently, he asked the chairman of Clacton Urban District Council, councillor O. B. Thompson, to perform the opening ceremony and donated all profits from the first four days to local charities, including Clacton Hospital, Clacton Unemployment Centre and the Clacton branch of the National Lifeboat Institution.

The pleasure park was an enormous success. Not only did it provide many thrilling rides, such as swing boats which turned right over, a gravity glide, dodgems, the loop-o-plane and the big 'Eli' wheel, the largest in the country, but it also put on many freak shows and speciality acts. The 'freaks' included the World's Largest Girl, a Living Skeleton, the Ice Maiden, the Rubber Man and the Black Man who could turn himself white. The freak show was advertised as 'NOTHING DISGUSTING! NOTHING DEGRADING!' The speciality acts included the Russian Cossacks, Dare-Devil Peggy, a 56-year-old one-legged diver who dived from a height of 65 feet enveloped in flames into a blazing cauldron five feet deep, and the Stratosphere Girl. The Stratosphere Girl, whose real name was Camilla Mayer, was one of the most remarkable and popular acts ever to appear in Clacton. It consisted of her performing extraordinary stunts perched on a two-inch wide platform on top of a steel pole 135 feet high. On this platform she would stand on her head, on her hands, or on one toe. She brought her act to its climax by sliding along a rope from the pole to the centre of the park holding on by her teeth. She was

105 *Dancing was always a popular pastime at Butlin's. This 1939 photograph shows dancing in the dining hall. After dinner all the tables and chairs were removed to make the necessary space.*

just 19 years of age when she first performed at Butlin's.

Meanwhile Billy Butlin was still conscious of the need to integrate fully into the town and to win over the many doubters that still existed, and throughout the 1937 season he continued to put on free stage shows in the park and to donate further large sums to local charities. He took a very active part in the Clacton Carnival and also organised a football team to take part in the local league. The club was so successful it won the Walton & District Charity Cup in its first season.

By the time the holiday camp itself opened, on 11 June 1938, Butlin's was already a familiar name in Clacton and what little opposition there still was had been effectively silenced by the overwhelming support now apparent for Billy Butlin throughout the town. He was providing the facilities and atmosphere to help turn Clacton into a booming

holiday resort and his public relations machine had been working overtime to ensure that he carried the people of Clacton with him. Furthermore he had ensured that local businesses were to benefit from the increased trade by signing contracts with local shops and firms to provide the goods and services necessary for the running of the camp. For example, T.H. Price of Rosemary Road supplied the greengrocery; Model Farm Dairies and Stetchworth Dairies the milk and dairy produce; the Princes Café bread, cakes and pastries, and Messrs Wright and Son, the High Street butchers, provided the meat, while Empire Films of Wellesley Road became the camp's official photographer.

The Holiday with Pay Act, invoked by Jack Shingfield as one of his arguments for supporting the building of the camp, passed through parliament and became law in 1938 just in time for the Camp's opening. This Act legally guaranteed one week's paid holiday per year to all industrial workers and gave an enormous boost to bookings. Butlin was able to advertise in the national press with the slogan: 'Holidays with pay; Holidays with play. A week's holiday for a week's wage.' He set the cost of a week's holiday at the camp at £3 10s., which was equal to the average week's wage at that time. Butlin organised a grand ceremonial opening to which he invited every one of the MPs who had voted in favour of the Holidays with Pay Act and laid on a special train to bring 200 VIPs down from London. The camp was officially opened by Lord Strabolgi, though it was left to another speaker, Lord Castlerosse, to verbalise the thoughts of all present when he solemnly announced that 'Billy Butlin has done more for England than St George.'

When first opened the camp provided accommodation for 1,000 holidaymakers. Although only four hundred arrived for the first week, the camp was fully booked for most of the season and further building was already under-way to provide an extra 500 places. From the start the entertainments manager, Mr Frank Cusworth (who had been one of Butlin's very first redcoats at Skegness), laid on an outstanding programme of entertainments and booked many of the country's leading stage and sports stars for appearances at the camp.

The programme for the first week went like this:

SATURDAY: Dance in Ballroom.

SUNDAY: Afternoon: Games and Tea Dance. Evening: Concert by Viennese Symphony Orchestra.

MONDAY: Day: Sporting Competitions. Evening: Whist Drive and Dance.

TUESDAY: Day: Crazy Cricket Match. Evening: Fancy Dress Carnival.

106   *Dancing in the much more elegant Viennese Ballroom, c.1960. Weekly ballroom dancing competitions were held at all Butlin's camps and the winners met in the finals held in London's Royal Albert Hall during the winter.*

WEDNESDAY: Day: Tennis Tournament, Boxing & Wrestling. Evening: Ladies Night when ladies take over duties of gentlemen by inviting the gentlemen to dance or paying for their refreshment. (The *Clacton Times and East Essex Gazette* of 18 June 1938 reported that "this, of course, caused great fun.")

THURSDAY: Day: Tennis Tournament, Field Sports and Table Tennis Tournament. Evening: Concert given by Campers.

FRIDAY: Day: Cricket Match and Fancy Dress Parade. Evening: Weekly Grand Farewell Carnival Dance.

The highlight of the first season came during the week of 3-9 July, when a 'Festival of Holiday Health & Happiness' was held. This was open to non-residents as well as residents at a daily cost of 1s. Special events included exhibition boxing by the British light heavyweight champion, Len Harvey, exhibition tennis by Dan Maskell, a snooker tournament for the grand prize of 100 guineas between Joe Davis and Horace Lindrum, and a demonstration of ballroom dancing by Mr and Mrs Victor Sylvester. The whole week culminated in a concert broadcast live on the BBC starring Elsie and Doris Waters, Vic Oliver, George Robey, Will Fyffe, Hildegaarde, Lew Stone and Mantovani with his Tipica Orchestra.

Other well-known stars to appear at Butlin's that season included Gracie Fields, Albert Whelan, the Stratosphere Girl, Marion Crowley ('Clacton's Shirley Temple') and Dennis Gilbert (at 13 years of age, billed as 'The world's youngest dancing xylophonist'). As well as the tournaments, exhibitions, concerts and dancing, Butlin's also laid on daily keep fit classes plus expert tuition in such sports as boxing, swimming and tennis. Religion was not forgotten. A large Sunday Service was held every week presided over by the Rev. H.G. Redgrave, the vicar of St James', in whose parish the camp lay. He acted as camp chaplain.

So integrated had the camp become into the life of the town that during that first season the *Clacton Times and East Essex Gazette* carried a weekly page reporting on happenings in the camp. It noted all the stars who were appearing and printed interesting snippets of life in the camp. For example, the following appeared on 3 September,

Campers will be interested to know that Miss K. Hartley of Maida Vale, W9, who has been on holiday at the camp is increasing her weight. Some time ago she wrote to a national newspaper stating that despite the fact that she eats 5 rashers of bacon, 2 eggs and 4 thick slices of toast for breakfast, her figure remains as slim as ever. The camp management thereupon wrote to her challenging her to sample the cooking of Joe Velich, the 22-stone chef, who would see if he could fatten her. He has evidently succeeded despite the fact that she has been doing a lot of exercise.

The *Gazette* also carried the results of all the competitions held in the camp including the bathing beauty, whist drive, putting, fancy dress (of which we learn that third prize in the humorous section for the week ending 23 July went to Messrs Irving and Slapp for their portrayal of 'Rinso'), swimming, tennis, table tennis and field sports (including the egg and spoon and three-legged races). For these sporting events the campers were divided into two houses – South and North – and points were scored for their houses by the winners of the competitions. During that first season North won the cup every week until 10 September.

At the end of the season the *Gazette* was able to report that the camp had been a 'greater success than ever imagined', both in terms of the camp itself and its acceptance into the town. There was, however, one small gripe. All Butlin's vegetables were imported from the farm in Lincolnshire which supplied the Skegness Camp. 'Is there any special reason why the lorry should travel from Lincolnshire (300 miles there and back) with the campers' dinners?' the *East Essex Gazette* demanded to know.

Following the closure of the camp to holidaymakers for the season, Billy Butlin decided to open its doors to Clacton residents on Wednesday and Saturday evenings. This was a service to the townspeople which continued until well after the Second World War and one which is still fondly remembered by many Clacton inhabitants as the high spot of their social week.

Enlarged to take 2,000 campers, Butlin's opened for the 1939 season at Whitsun of that year having already attracted 30,000 day visitors on to the camp over the Easter weekend. New improvements for the 1939 season included 1,000 rose trees, a bowling green, six new shops, open-air roller-skating, a miniature railway and an £8,000 electric organ installed in the new dance hall.

Not only was the camp going from strength to strength but so too was its football team which came top of the first division of the Essex and Suffolk Border league. Their aim eventually was to turn professional. Life at the camp carried on much as the 1938 season; Len Harvey and Mantovani were again regular visitors. Other stars such as Syd Walker, Stainless Stephen and Claire Luce appeared. On 2 June 1939 Butlin's was again able to demonstrate its commitment to Clacton when it sent along its own fire tender to help at the Lewellen's fire.

As Britain slipped closer and closer to war with Germany minor disruptions upset the smooth running of the camp. The tannoy system was continually interrupting its entertainment broadcasts to give the names of men who had to report back to their home town for call-up. Practice black-outs were held on the camp and, worst of all from Butlin's point of view, reservists, school teachers and air-raid wardens were told to cancel their holidays altogether. Billy Butlin himself refused to believe there was going to be a war, and he had the camp newspaper, *Butlin Times*, run the headline 'Bye-bye blues at Butlin's? Campers forget the crisis. Are we downhearted? No!!', and he ran an interview with

one of his holidaymakers who said, 'There is time enough to worry if and when war comes, and I'm certainly not going to let Hitler mess up my holiday.'

On the morning war was declared, 3 September, Butlin was actually in the Clacton camp calming the campers and reassuring them that there wasn't going to be a war! As soon as war was declared the camp was emptied and it was handed over first to the Air Force and then to the Army for use as an internment camp. Some chalets were demolished to allow a barbed-wire perimeter fence to be erected, with floodlights every few yards. However,

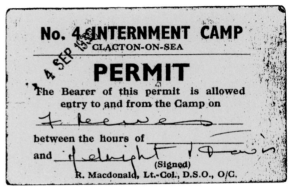

107   *When the Second World War broke out in 1939, Butlin's became an internment camp. This is a pass issued to Butlin official Frank Reeves, to allow him onto the site.*

as there weren't many internees the camp was soon given to the Royal Auxiliary Corps, later the Pioneer Corps. The Army continued at the camp in one form or another until the war ended, when it was handed back to Butlin's. It was ready in time to open for the 1946 season and did so on 6 April with 800 guests. Even on that very first weekend, after six years occupation by the military, a number of top stars were lined up to entertain the campers. There was the mind reader and hypnotist Maurice Fogel, Wally Goodman the comedian and Terry Thomas, billed as an impressionist.

The *East Essex Gazette* of 12 April took its readers on a tour of the camp:

108   *The Royal Auxiliary Corps (later the Pioneer Corps) marching into the camp in 1940.*

[There are] rows of brightly coloured chalets with gardens between each row. There are shops, a post office and 'Radio Butlin's'. A gay nursery with toys and rocking horses is provided for the children who are all labelled to ensure they do not get lost. For casualties there is a sick ward. What was formerly the sergeant's mess is now a bar – the Jolly Roger … The ballroom, one of the finest in England, has protruding fairy tale castles as the walls and Tudor pillars supporting a centre balcony … The dining room has plastic table cloths of many colours; food is brought in on electrically-heated trolleys. There is a splendid gym with a boxing ring. Indoor entertainments include a theatre, billiards room and sun lounge and out-of-doors there are tennis courts, a bowling green, swimming pool and fountain … In the mornings 'Cappie' Bond and an army instructor take voluntary P.T. classes, while a sympathetic trainer takes the children.

Following advertisements in the local press for staff, including typists, clerks, waiters, waitresses, cooks, kitchen hands, chalet maids, cleaners and handymen, the camp was inundated with 17,000 applications for jobs, of which 550 were successful. For most of the rest of the first post-war season, Butlin's was full and the camp took up more or less exactly where it had left off in 1939 except that the *Gazette* no longer devoted a whole page to happenings there. There was no question now that it was part of Clacton, though there was still the odd minor hiccup as when the amusement park manager was fined £1 for 'using a musical instrument worked by mechanical means (i.e. a hurdy-gurdy) to be played to the annoyance of residents between June 1st and 3rd'.

The period between 1946 and the early 1960s were the halcyon days of the holiday camp and Butlin's at Clacton was no exception. After six years of war people were looking for the opportunity to let their hair down and enjoy themselves; holiday camps gave that opportunity. They were not too expensive and everything was provided for one all-in cost. Food, entertainments, amusements, competitions, even a chalet maid to make your bed was all paid for at the outset. In theory you could go to Butlin's with no money at all in your pocket and still have a good time (though perhaps the local shopkeepers would not have approved too much).

Special clubs to cater for children were formed – the Beaver Club and the 913 Club. These provided their own activities and allowed their hard-pressed parents time off to enjoy themselves on their holiday in their own way. This was the era of the knobbly knees, the glamorous grandmother, the Tarzan look-alike and the spaghetti-eating competitions. The pre-war favourites such as the fancy dress competitions and the field sports also

109 *On 1 September 1946 the Grand Order of Water Rats visited the camp to give an 'all-star variety concert' which included Bud Flanagan, Will Fyffe, Nat Jackley, Talbot O'Farrell, Arthur Prince and Ben Warriss.*

110 *Eric Winstone was Butlin's resident band in the late 1940s and 1950s. His most famous composition was a song called 'Stagecoach'.*

111 *Shops were built on the camp in 1939 to cater for the campers' every need. This photograph taken in the early 1950s shows the hairdressers, fruit shop, post office and newsagent amongst others. These shops were later closed and amalgamated into one all-embracing supermarket-cum-departmental store.*

continued. The house competitions now became competitions between Kent House and Gloucester House, and later, as the camp grew, York House and Windsor House as well. There was fierce pride and loyalty to one's house. In the Summer 1992 issue of the *Clacton Chronicle* (the journal of the Clacton & District Local History Society), Roy Hudd, a Redcoat at Clacton in 1958, recounts the story of one event in which he was involved: 'I remember a very old lady being pushed, by me, in an inter house pram race. Suddenly we hit a bump in the road and the old darling catapulted out of the pram – landing on her head! We brought her round and her first words were "Did we win?!"'

Although the competitions seemed to charac-terise the success of Butlin's, it was ironically this form of activity which drew the most criticism of a Butlin's holiday after the war. There were com-plaints about 'strict regimentation' and having to join in the fun and games whether you wanted to

or not. As evidence the critics referred to the 'Wakey, Wakey' song played over the Radio Butlin tannoy at 7.30 every morning:

> Roll out of bed in the morning
> With a big, big smile and a good, good morning.
> You'll find life is worth while
> If you roll out of bed with a smile.

There were strict meal times with different sittings for Gloucester House, Kent House, etc., the con-tinual announcements on Radio Butlin about what activity was now taking place, the rôle of the Redcoats in organising the campers to take part, and so on, right up to the 'Goodnight Campers' song at 11.45 p.m.:

> Goodnight campers, see you in the morning;
> Goodnight campers I can see you yawning …
> Goodnight campers, goodnight.

Defenders of Butlin's pointed out that of course all the games and activities were laid on, but campers

112 *Happy campers at the poolside watching the swimming gala in August 1955. The boy just to the left of centre in the second row from the bottom looks as though he may grow up to write books about Clacton-on-Sea one day.*

113 *A popular method of travel around the camp and, indeed, around the streets of Clacton was the two-seater cycle. These riders are taking part in the Butlin's section of the 1958 Carnival Procession.*

could take part, watch or ignore them as they wished. No one was 'forced' to do anything. Billy Butlin himself made the point that after the war no one would have stood for any more regimentation; it was exactly what everyone was trying to get away from. For most women it meant a week's freedom they had never experienced before. As people became more affluent through the 1950s more and more families were going on holiday and enjoying the luxury of being waited on hand and foot. Meals were laid on, chalets were cleaned, beds made, and nurseries were provided. Chalet patrols listened out for crying babies at night. It was not regimentation that Butlin's brought. It was freedom on a scale undreamed of by most people in the 1930s, when the nearest many got to a holiday was to go hop picking in Kent or on other types of working holiday – if they went at all.

In his book, *The Englishman's Holiday*, J.A.R. Pimlott reports on a visit made to Butlin's at Clacton on 29 August 1946. This is what he had to say about the question of regimentation:

> I saw little evidence of regimentation or organised 'jollying' and heard little of 'Radio Butlin'. The proportion of campers engaged on anything active was small ... There were no 'hi-de-hi's and 'ho-de-ho's ... The company looked unremarkable – a good solid mixture of respectable people of all ages with none of the ostentatious jollity of which I had read.

One interesting sidelight on a holiday just after the war is provided by Pimlott's observation that most of the announcements Radio Butlin did make were that 'campers whose names began with certain letters should take their ration books along between such and such hours' to the office.

114   *One of Butlin's most popular competitions, the Holiday Princess. The prize in this 1960 photograph was awarded by Jim Musgrove, winner of Butlin's John O'Groats to Land's End walking race earlier that year.*

115 *A 1962-3 Clacton Winter Social Club card. The camp had first opened its doors to local residents at the end of the 1938 season.*

On the day that Pimlott was at Clacton he saw several star names at the camp. The resident band, the Squadronnaires, were there, as well as Harry Davidson and his orchestra, who played dance music in the ballroom at 9 p.m. and again at 10.45 p.m. Reggie Meen, the former British heavyweight boxing champion, gave an exhibition bout in the gym at 8 p.m. Many who were later to be stars and household names had some of their early entertaining experience at Butlin's Clacton either as

Redcoats or as resident singers and comedians. The Beverley Sisters, Michael Holliday, Des O'Connor, Jack Douglas, Ted Rogers, Charlie Drake, Dave Allen, Roy Hudd and Cliff Richard, who had his first ever professional engagement at Butlin's Clacton, all appeared at the camp in their younger days, while big stars of the time such as Arthur English, Tommy Trinder, Charlie Chester and Ted Ray also continued to appear. For many years in the 1940s and '50s the resident band was under the direction of Eric Winstone, already a well-established name in show business. Sports stars of the magnitude of Maurice Tate (cricket), John Pullman (snooker and billiards) and Jimmy Hill (football) continued the Butlin tradition of coaching.

By the late 1950s, Butlin's had become a national institution and, to some extent, Clacton was able to bask in its reflected glory. The combination of Butlin's and Clacton had become firmly established and the futures of both as family holiday venues seemed unshakeable. But the glory days of Butlin's were not to last for ever, and during the 1960s the process of change which would eventually

116 *The Regency Lounge in the late '60s, one of the many bars on the camp. For some reason staff were not allowed into this bar, even when off duty.*

117 *A view of the amusement park in 1966. All rides were free to campers and day visitors.*

118 *A general view of the chalets and gardens, c.1970.*

119 *Clacton was the first Butlin's camp to open at Christmas, which it did in 1938. The management forgot to lay on any heating! This view dates from around 1970 and shows resident children's comic, Uncle Tommy, with Father Christmas. Uncle Tommy used to sign autographs as 'Tommy Clown Uncle'. I can personally vouch for this if anyone wishes to see my autograph book!*

lead to Butlin's closure and Clacton's decline as a leading seaside resort gathered pace. The very affluence which had led many families to sample the delights of a week's holiday for the first time in their lives by choosing Butlin's was now to lead them to eschew the very idea of going to a holiday camp.

Most of Butlin's trade had come from the East End of London, a mere 75 miles away, and most of the rest from the Midlands, Birmingham and Leicester in particular. Two weeks holiday became increasingly the norm, and with the extra time people wanted to go further afield. Travelling abroad to Ostend, Paris or Spain was now within the budget of many families. British resorts were hard put to retain their clientele. Many campers who had returned year after year to Butlin's at Clacton with an unswerving loyalty were now beginning to desert the camp as the British way of life began to change. Somehow Butlin's seemed out of tune with the modern affluent style of the times and no match for the 'exotic' continent. In the 1960s the same

food was being served as had always been served but four heavy meals a day was now looked on as decidedly unhealthy. The accommodation was basically the same as when the camp opened in 1938, only now the chalets were beginning to look dilapidated and old. The jolly Redcoats leading the fun and games on the centre green or in the Viennese Ballroom was not in keeping with the individualism of the Swinging Sixties. The whole idea of organised fun and games was out of step with the current thinking of 'doing your own thing'.

By 1968, when Billy Butlin retired, family groups at the camp had fallen to an all-time low. Their place had been taken by large groups of single teenagers who, for the first time, had plenty of money in their pockets and were able to spend it largely as they pleased. Ironically, this new generation discovered all over again that Butlin's gave them the freedom they desired and allowed them to escape from the disciplines of home, school and work. In a manner of speaking, the wheel had come full circle, but this time the new chairman of

120 *A 1970 view of Butlin's main street with the Gaiety Theatre on the right. After the camp was demolished in the 1980s two of the soldiers seen above the entrance to the theatre were saved and are now the proud possessions of Tendring District Council.*

121 *This is what Butlin's is all about! Fun and games on the playing fields, c.1970.*

122 *Sunbathing in front of the outdoor swimming pool, c.1970.*

123 *The paddling pool next to the main swimming pool, c.1970.*

Butlin's, Billy's son Bobby, was concerned that the new-style freedom had gone too far. The camp's reputation reached an all time low as teenagers, perhaps for the first time in their lives, discovered a place where they could indulge in excesses of drink and sex with very little control over their activities. There were stories of all-night parties, drinking, vandalism, gang-fights and chalet-swapping. Those families still wishing to come were reluctant to get caught up in this experience and in 1965, for the first time since it opened its first camp in Skegness in 1936, Butlin's as a whole lost business.

Bobby Butlin moved swiftly to restore the reputation and fortunes of the company and immediately stopped block bookings from single teenagers. But he realised he needed more than just a negative approach if he was to entice families back to Clacton. He launched a programme of modernisation, building chalets with private bathrooms and converting large numbers of existing chalets, equipping them with cookers and fridges to provide self-catering holidays. For those campers who still wished to eat their meals in the dining hall, Butlin's now only provided breakfast and an evening meal. Fast food outlets were opened on the camp and campers were given the option of eating the meals provided in the dining hall, buying them at one of the retail outlets or cooking their own. The wearing of badges, an outward sign of the outdated regimentation, was also stopped. These changes had their effect, bookings picked up and in 1971 Butlin's enjoyed a record year.

However, more changes to the familiar style of the holiday camp were just over the horizon. In 1972 Butlin's was taken over by the Rank Organisation, and in 1977 they scrapped the 'Wakey Wakey' song over the tannoy which had called generations of Clacton campers to their breakfast. The Redcoats were also given a new rôle as times changed. The old house system was abolished and the camp merely divided into red camp and blue camp, to differentiate between the self-catering guests and the half-board guests, so the redcoat as partisan house supporter urging the campers on to superhuman efforts to gain house points had to change, and they became the up-front public relations representatives of the Butlin's organisation

124 *Although Butlin's is thought of primarily as a holiday centre, it was, of course, the workplace for anything up to 1,000 staff during the summer, most of whom belonged to the Transport and General Workers' Union. This photograph, taken during the 1978 season, shows the TGWU General Secretary Jack Jones, on the left, with Len Hanks, the regional secretary, meeting the local Branch Secretary, Percy Ward.*

125 *The front cover of the Butlin's programme for the week of the Royal Wedding in 1981. On the day of the wedding itself, additional television sets were situated in the Viennese Ballroom and the South Seas Lounge Bar for the campers' 'convenience'.*

dispensing information and goodwill. They were no longer forced to crack jokes every second of the day!

This is not to say, of course, that games and other activities were no longer organised, but knobbly knees and glamorous grandmothers apart, all the old Butlin's style had gone to be replaced by normal – and generally more healthy – pursuits. A typical week's programme from the late 1970s and 80s looked something like this:

SUNDAY: Morning: Billiards tournament, snooker coaching, national pentathlete award scheme. Afternoon: Swimming gala, whist drive. Evening: Modern sequence and old tyme dancing, national pentathlete swimming tests, old tyme music hall.

MONDAY: Morning: Cricket coaching, darts coaching. Afternoon: Its-a-Knockout tournament, cricket coaching. Evening: Music and entertainment in the Blinking Owl Bar, knobbly knees contest.

TUESDAY: Morning: Table tennis tournament, snooker coaching. Afternoon: Donkey derby, cricket coaching, five-a-side soccer. Evening: Dancing, cabaret.

126 *A publicity photograph for Butlin's last ever season at Clacton, 1983.*

WEDNESDAY: Morning: National pent-athlete tests, sports brain quiz. Afternoon: Five-a-side soccer, cash bingo. Evening: Butlin's star - trial heats, disco dancing.

THURSDAY: Morning: Putting tournament, dancing instruction. Afternoon: Family sports, glamorous grandmother competition. Evening: Rock & pop club, vocal contest.

FRIDAY: Morning: Snooker, cricket coaching. Afternoon: Five-a-side soccer, cricket coaching. Evening: Highlights of the week's events shown on the giant video screen, farewell dance in the Viennese Ballroom.

(Taken from the 1982 season programme)

By 1980 Butlin's had again reached new heights, with yet another record year for visitors. Thanks to a continual programme of building, the original 1,000 capacity of Clacton Camp had grown to 6,000 and everything looked set for a bright future. As the camp closed its doors on the 1983 season there was no hint of the disaster to come. Seasonal staff were offered contracts for the following season and in the current edition of *Butlin News*, Peter Wilson, the bookings manager for Clacton, said he was looking forward to 1985, 'the year in which he expects to get a computer to sort out his allocation section'. But in the offices of the Rank Organisation changes were being dreamt up to streamline and modernise Butlin's. Holiday Camps were a thing of the past. The word camp gave the wrong image of the modern holiday, so whole new 'holiday centres' and 'holiday villages' were to be created. All chalets were now to be the height of luxury, with wall-to-wall carpeting, colour televisions, teasmaids and private bathrooms. To pay for these improvements Rank decided that something had to go, and that something was the camps at Filey and Clacton.

In a press statement Bobby Butlin summed up the decision by saying that a review had been carried out 'with a view to planning for the future development of Butlin's. As a result it was decided that

127 *This was how seasonal staff were told the camp had closed for ever. The letter is undated but is from October 1983.*

these two centres are no longer viable and regrettably they must close. We deeply regret having to take this painful decision and the effect that the closure will have on the staff of both centres and on the community.' It was the end of an era for Clacton, brought about by a corporate investment decision based on hard economic facts with little time for nostalgia or the local impact of that decision. The closure meant the loss of 100 permanent jobs and 841 seasonal jobs, a devastating blow to a town which already had one of the highest rates of unemployment in south-east England.

In 1936 and 1937 there had been much controversy in the town about whether to allow Butlin

128   *And this is what eventually took Butlin's place, the Martello Bay housing estate. This is a view down Hastings Avenue where the camp entrance used to be.*

to build his camp on the West Clacton estate. No voices were raised to say it was a good thing Butlin's was pulling out. The town was shocked and angry at the decision. It was again left to the leading Labour Party councillor, Roy Smith, to put that anger into words. In a bitter attack on the Rank Organisation he said that Butlin's had made no attempt to make improvements at the camp. 'They have creamed off the income from the town and left us stranded. It is deplorable. I am very concerned about the attitude of Butlin's in recent years. This closure has been brought about by Butlin's themselves not putting enough back into the town.' Butlin's denied these allegations, pointing out that as recently as 1977 they had invested £2 million at Clacton: 'We are certainly not creaming anything off the town. The reverse was true. The town was creaming off us because of the number of holiday-makers and day visitors we brought into the town.' The carefully nurtured co-operation between camp and town had finally disintegrated into this acrimonious exchange as Butlin's departure virtually destroyed the last vestiges of Clacton's one-time reputation as a leading British holiday resort.

IX

Post-War Clacton

WHEN WAR BROKE out Clacton was at first considered to be a safe haven and mothers and children were evacuated to the area from London. However, two incidents occurred in 1940 which moved the town into the front line and instead of evacuees coming to Clacton the traffic went the other way and the population dropped from 24,000 to 5,000. First the pier was badly damaged by a floating mine in February, the explosion also smashing hotel and house windows in town, while a column of black smoke, 100 feet high, could be seen from miles away. The second incident occurred

129 *When the Second World War started evacuees came to Clacton from London. This photograph, from May 1940, shows mothers and children arriving from north London to be billeted in St Osyth Road.*

on the night of 20 April 1940 when a German plane on a mine-laying mission was shot down over Harwich and circled round in ever-decreasing circles, eventually crashing to the ground in Victoria Road, Clacton. The residents of number 25, Mr and Mrs Frederick Gill, were killed outright and became the first civilian casualties of the war anywhere in England.

Clacton suffered further damage through the war, in particular in May 1941 when the old Town Hall was badly damaged by a lone raider and the Town Hall clock had to be pulled down and demolished. In all Clacton endured 1,084 air-raid alerts. With the lifting of wartime restrictions in 1944, the town hoped to regain its place at the top of the seaside tree, and although the late '40s and '50s were to show that Clacton was once again a popular holiday destination, it was never to be quite

the same. Two of the biggest hotels, the *Towers* and the *Grand* closed for business. In fact, the *Towers* never opened at all after the war, while the *Grand*, struggled on for a couple of seasons before closing its doors for ever. Both hotels became part of St Osyth's Teacher Training College. The *East Essex Gazette* warned that 'for the best sites on the Marine Parade to be occupied by a training college is an economic disaster'. Only three of the six cinemas re-opened, while, on the pier, the Children's Theatre and the Crystal Casino had disappeared for good.

Nevertheless, visitors were still flocking to the town, and on August Bank Holiday 1950 it was reported that 21,100 rail passengers had arrived to add to the thousands coming by coach. In 1952 the council decided to make an all-out effort to attract visitors and appointed a new Publicity Manager to mastermind a new campaign. Harry Thompson,

130 *(left)   Following the explosions on the pier and in Victoria Road, however, traffic was soon going the other way. This is Mr Learoyd (at the back), the headmaster of St Osyth Road School, with some of his pupils getting ready to evacuate to the West Country.*

131 *(above)   This is all that was left of the old Town Hall after a lone German raider dropped a bomb on the corner of Station Road and Rosemary Road in May 1941.*

132 *(right)   Clacton's Home Guard was formed in May 1940 as the Local Defence Volunteers. Within two days of their formation, 500 men had registered at Clacton police station. They were finally stood down at the end of 1944. The menu for the celebration dinner seems to owe much to its wartime context as it consisted of 'Meat Soup, Tongue and Spam, Apple Pie and Coffee'.*

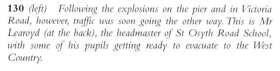

NO. 6 PLATOON
'B' COMPANY, 17th BATTALION
ESSEX HOME GUARD.

DINNER
and
SOCIAL EVENING

AT THE
TOWN HALL, CLACTON-ON-SEA
FRIDAY, OCTOBER 27th, 1944

TO COMMEMORATE
THE STANDING DOWN
OF
THE HOME GUARD

133 (left)   A scene from one of Harry Thompson's publicity tours. This was Sheffield in 1956.

134 (right)   As part of the CUDC's publicity drive, Clacton used to enter floats in other town's Carnival Processions. This float won first prize in the Hendon Borough Carnival in 1953. No expense was spared to obtain the most glamorous girls. From left to right: 'Miss English Rose', Brenda Mee, 'Miss Great Britain', Marlene Dee, and 'Miss Bikini of the World', Laura Ellison-Davis.

135 (below right)   The Clacton Carnival remained very popular throughout the post-war period. This is a scene from the 1953 Carnival showing the CUDC's own float passing near the Venetian Bridge.

the man given the job, set about organising a winter tour to publicise the delights of Clacton. Appointed in February, by April he had already visited Birmingham, Coventry, Leicester, Nottingham, London, Oxford and Reading. By the end of the year traders in Southend were complaining that 'Clacton is getting more and more popular and is taking all our trade away from us'.

His tours were undertaken in a coach donated by Premier Travel, who had a vested interest in the outcome as they were the only coach company to provide a direct route to Clacton from the Midlands and the North. In 1952 they applied to run a direct service to Nottingham. In their application they said that during 1951 they had brought 600 visitors from Leicester on their weekly service and that many more enquiries had been received from other Midlands towns.

NSHINE · GOLDEN SANDS
· CHAMPAGNE AIR ·

With an improving rail service, the 'hourly interval' service of semi-fast trains was introduced in 1950, and several coach companies, including Grey Green, Eastern National and Sutton's, vying for the business from London, Clacton was still well served by public transport, although the regular Saturday morning bottleneck at the Mark's Tey roundabout did tend to put a damper on the road experience.

The 1950s was a good era for Clacton. An estimated 100,000 visitors arrived over the 1955 August Bank Holiday. It was said at the time that there were so many people on Clacton beach that the tide couldn't get in! The pier was as popular as ever. Now run by Barney Kingsman, following his father's death at the end of the war, the Pavilion, renamed the Jolly Roger, was putting on nightly shows, as was the Ocean Theatre, while the Ramblas

138 *A packed section of the West Beach in the mid-1950s, showing the pleasure boat, Nemo II,* taking on board passengers for a trip round the Pier. The Nemo *served Clacton holidaymakers from 1928 until 1982.*

136 *The new semi-fast hourly Interval Service arrives at Clacton in 1950.*

137 *Clacton Urban District Council always liked to make a good first impression on visitors and kept the gardens opposite the railway station in immaculate condition, as can be seen in this photograph dating from the late 1950s.*

were performing open-air daytime revues. The Steel Stella was still thrilling the youngsters, while for even younger children there was the Cresta Run helter-skelter and the Peter Pan Railway. The swimming pool and the Blue Lagoon, with dancing to Teddy Dobbs and his orchestra, were still popular attractions.

With Ronnie Mills as resident band leader at the Band Pavilion, crowds were flocking in their thousands. Dance bands had long since taken over from the military band as a seaside attraction, and some of the world's top bands appeared with Ronnie Mills, including Ray Connif, Ted Heath and Mantovani. The Pavilion was also the setting for other

139 *Another view of the West Beach dating from the late '50s, showing the Punch & Judy stand of Claude North Junior.*

140 *One of the last of the old-style paddle steamers to visit Clacton on a regular basis was the* Golden Eagle, *built in 1909 and scrapped in 1951. Its last Clacton season was 1950. This view dates from 1949.*

forms of entertainment, including the Evening Standard Fashion Show and the Clacton Ideal Holiday Girl contest. The Ideal Holiday Girl was another of Harry Thompson's brainwaves and he organised heats throughout the country on his winter tours. This ensured plenty of national publicity when the finals were held. The theatres were still booking some of the country's top stars. Tony Hancock starred in a summer season at the Ocean Theatre in 1950, while Max Miller, Alma Cogan, Dickie Valentine and Billy Cotton all headlined at the Savoy Theatre (the old Operetta House) for a week each in 1959.

But towards the end of the 1950s there were the first signs that things might not always be this good. The West Cliff Theatre ran into trouble in 1958 and had to be bailed out by the council, and in 1959, for the first time since the London Concert

141 *An aerial view of the pier, c.1960, showing some of the many entertainments still going strong, including the Jolly Roger, the Ramblas Open Air Theatre, the Ocean Theatre, the Steel Stella, the Cresta Run helter-skelter, the Swimming Pool, the Dodgems and the Blue Lagoon Dance Hall.*

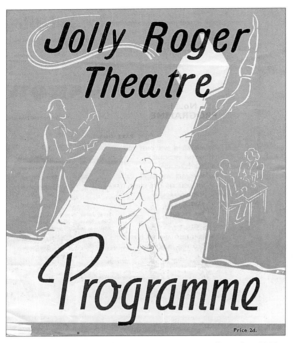

142 *A Jolly Roger Theatre programme cover from the 1958 season. The show was 'Show Time' and starred the Ramblas.*

Company had moved to the West Cliff site in 1899, no shows were put on while its future was decided. In the end the council bought the theatre and it was saved, but it was a timely reminder. By the 1960s a change was coming over the habits of British holidaymakers. The country in general was becoming more affluent and more and more employers were granting longer periods of paid holiday. The idea of a week at Clacton was no longer the acme of ambition and people were looking to holidays abroad. In 1962 the Kinema Grand cinema was demolished, while in 1963 the *Grosvenor Court* hotel was destroyed by fire, never to reopen.

But far worse was to come in 1964. This was the year of the infamous Mods and Rockers riot. It all started quietly enough on Good Friday when a trickle of teenagers on motor scooters (mods) began to arrive in Clacton. As it happens they had come to Clacton to listen to the entertainment

143 *The 1964 Ramblas Concert Party. This was the last year they were to perform in Clacton, having been regular end-of-the-pier entertainers since 1936. On the extreme left of the photograph is Gordon Henson, star and producer of the show.*

which had been laid on specially for the Easter holiday by Clacton Council, who were trying to promote the town as a lively seaside resort for youngsters and were pleased, at first, that the teenagers were arriving to try it out. The bands lined up for that week-end included Johnny Pilgrim and the Classics, Shane Fenton and the Fentones and, one of the biggest names in the country at that time, Freddie and the Dreamers. During the day, the mods began to make their way to camps on the outskirts of town at Holland, Jaywick and by the airstrip. Later on a smaller number of teenagers on motor cycles (rockers) began to appear. The mods and rockers were sworn enemies and whenever two large groups appeared in one place it was almost inevitable that trouble would follow. On Saturday the numbers arriving grew from a trickle into a torrent and the scene was set for the violence that was to engulf Clacton over the next three days.

The first clashes came in Pier Avenue just after midnight and the police arrived to try and stop the riot. But if there was one thing the mods and rockers hated more than each other it was the police, so from then on the gang warfare was largely forgotten as the two groups turned their attention to the police and fighting continued throughout the night. After a brief lull just before dawn, violence flared up again on Sunday with windows in the Pavilion being smashed. Just after lunch there was something like a thousand youngsters milling about around the Marine Parade/Pier Avenue junction. There were dozens of arrests and the gangs began to break up. By Monday things had calmed down although sporadic outbreaks of violence were still being reported.

The newspapers had a field day and Clacton hit the nation's headlines for all the wrong reasons. The *Daily Mail* said 'Clacton represents a new high-water mark in hooliganism', and the *Daily Mirror* spoke of 'an orgy of unholy hooliganism … by idiotic teenagers on the rampage'. In fact, the events

144   *During the 1950s the M.V.* Queen of the Channel *used to make regular trips from the pier to France.*

of that weekend were nowhere near as bad as the press portrayed it. The police denied that the trouble had ever got out of hand and only 12 youngsters were prosecuted. Leslie Price, owner of the *Waverley Hotel* at the time, summed it up when he said,

The whole event was exaggerated. When you see large numbers of anyone you are bound to feel intimidated. 300 farmers strung across a road for example, but especially leather-jacketed youngsters. Of course you felt queasy walking down the street between them, but nothing happened to bystanders. I didn't see any violence or examples of anti-social behaviour. There were stories in the press about a break in at the

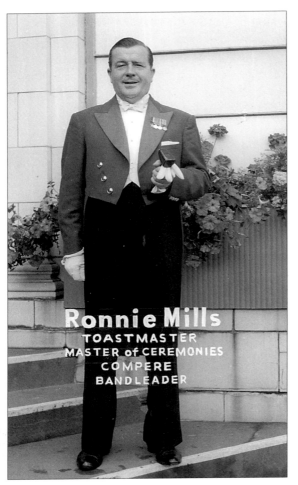

145 *Ronnie Mills, Clacton's most popular entertainer throughout the 1950s and '60s. His was the resident band at the Band Pavilion throughout most of that period.*

Waverley Hotel. This was completely untrue. There were a number trying to get in to use the toilet and we let them in two or three at a time. There was no trouble. In fact, most people in Clacton didn't know anything was happening. It was only when they were rung up by relatives who had seen it on the news or heard it on the radio they realised anything was going on! It was a quiet weekend for world news and the papers just latched on to it.

Whatever the truth, many families cancelled their holidays for the 1964 season, and there is no doubt that the events of that Easter weekend accelerated

the decline of Clacton as a leading seaside resort. Of course it was not the only reason and, things were changing anyway, but it certainly did not help.

In spite of the falling holiday trade, Clacton continued to expand as the population grew. Much of the influx was retired people. The proportion of those of pensionable age living in Clacton rose from 23.6 per cent in 1951 to 32 per cent in 1961, and then in the next decade to 1971 to 39 per cent. For those people still of working age, new employment had to be found to take the place of tourism-based jobs and a number of new industrial estates grew up, such as Oxford Road and Gorse Lane, mostly catering for light engineering firms and other small businesses. In the meantime there were more signs of the waning popularity of Clacton as a seaside resort. In 1966 the *Oulton Hall Hotel* closed and joined the *Towers* and the *Grand* as part of the St Osyth's Training College. In 1967 the Clacton Cricket Festival ended and Essex stopped playing county games at Vista Road, and in 1971, in perhaps the most symbolic act of all, Barney Kingsman sold the pier.

The decline continued through the 1970s. In 1972 the *Ambleside Hotel* was demolished. In 1973 the Steel Stella was destroyed by fire and never rebuilt. In 1974 the *Warwick Castle Hotel* and the Palace Theatre were demolished. In 1978 the Ocean Theatre closed and Barney Kingsman died. By the 1980s very little was left to remind the world that Clacton-on-Sea had once been one of the country's leading seaside resorts and when Butlin's closed at the end of the 1983 season it seemed like the final

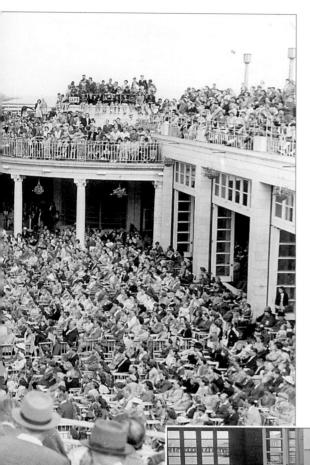

146 *A crowded Band Pavilion in the mid-'50s. Altogether the Pavilion could accommodate up to 3,000 spectators, and it was not unknown for this number to be reached on occasion. Here the audience is watching the Dagenham Girl Pipers.*

147 *The Band Pavilion was used for much more than just band concerts in the '50s and '60s. This is a photograph of the 1962 Evening Standard Fashion Show.*

nail in the coffin. To emphasise this, the Odeon Cinema also closed that year.

A consortium of former Butlin's managers bought the Butlin's site and the following year opened Atlas Park, an American-style theme park, but it was a failure and closed after just one year. The area remained empty and derelict for a while but was eventually turned over to housing and Clacton's prime holiday entertainment area, dating back to the Edwardian period, was lost for ever. The row of shops built on the empty Odeon Cinema site remained empty for over 18 months. In 1986 it was reported that Clacton had lost 66 per cent of its hotel places since 1966. What was even worse was that the national depression of the early '80s was having a big impact on Clacton and its recently developed light engineering industry.

148 *Paul Raymond brought a dash of Parisian glamour to Clacton when he took over the Savoy Theatre in the early 1960s.*

149 *The Penguins Repertory Company put on seasons at a number of the town's theatres during the 1950s and '60s, including the Savoy, the West Cliff and the Princes. This photograph is taken outside the Princes.*

150 *A popular attraction put on in 1955 to draw in the tourists was the Clacton Coach Rally. This is the crowded scene on Clacton greensward. Eighty-two coaches took part, coming from as far away as Liskeard in Cornwall, Sheffield and Cheltenham. Among the judges were Kenneth Horne and Raymond Baxter.*

151 *The Essoldo Cinema in the early 1960s. In spite of several changes of name since it was founded as the Century in 1936, this is Clacton's only remaining cinema, now known as Flicks. At this period the cinema also put on midnight matinée stage shows with stars such as Max Bygraves and The Shadows.*

In fact, Clacton suffered greatly from high unemployment, reaching over 20 per cent by the mid-
'80s and it became one of the South East's black
spots.

   As if to sum up Clacton's precarious position,
part of the wall facing St John's Church tower
collapsed in 1990 and the oldest building in the
town had to be closed to worshippers for the first
time since it was built in the 12th century. That
event seemed to mark the low point of Clacton's
fortunes and, since then, the town has slowly but
surely fought back and there have been a number
of promising and optimistic signs throughout the
'90s to show that the holiday trade has been making
a comeback and that the town is far from finished.
In 1994 the Harrison family bought the pier, which
had once again been in receivership, and began to
inject millions of pounds into it in an attempt to
return it to something like it was in the Kingsman
era. In 1996 the area around the Band Pavilion was
completely revamped by local businessman, Billy
Peak, with fast food outlets and new amusements
opened up to the public. In 1999 a half-million
pound scheme to redesign and modernise the sea-

152   *Another popular children's facility in Clacton was the model
yacht pond opposite the Palace. This is a late 1950s view.*

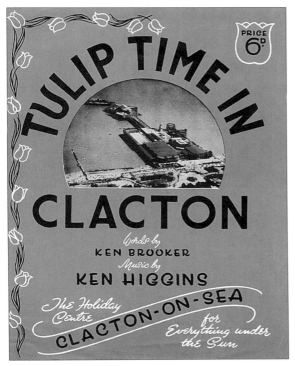

front gardens and to build a new children's play area was completed with the help of lottery money. As if to emphasise this resurgence, a large and expansive public building, the new Police Station, was opened in 1997 as a reminder of that proud period in the late '20s and early '30s when the school, railway station and Town Hall were built.

But it was maybe the old village of Great Clacton that finally had the last laugh at Clacton's

153 (left)   *Believe it or not, there have been a number of songs written especially for Clacton. One was 'Sunny Clacton', written by Teddy Dobbs in the 1930s, and this one, 'Tulip Time in Clacton', was written by Ken Brooker and Ken Higgins in the 1950s.*

154 (below left)   *A view of Pier Avenue and Electric Parade, c.1959, just about the time when the name Electric Parade fell into disuse.*

155 (below)   *This is how the local paper, the* East Essex Gazette *reported the Mods and Rockers riot in 1964.*

East Essex Gazette

No. 2536   FRIDAY, APRIL 3, 1964   PRICE FOURPENCE

CLACTON COUNTS LOSSES FROM EASTER TEENAGE INVASION

Whitsun pledge by police

Wanted— a queen

A street scene typical of Clacton town centre over the weekend, including a police dog-handler patrolling with Alsatian.

Takings are down by £60,000: Rates strike threat

CLACTON'S hoteliers and tradespeople reckon the cost of the Easter violence was at least £60,000 in cash takings over bars and counters, apart from the wanton damage to property and holiday bookings through bad publicity.

MENDED FOR BRIDE

NO TROUBLE WITH THESE TEENAGERS

inside pages

156 *A symbolic view of Clacton's post-war decline. This photograph, taken in the late 1930s, shows four of Clacton's large hotels. From left to right are the* Grand, *the* Towers, *the* Oulton Hall *and the* Hadleigh, *all of which became part of the Colchester Institute after the war.*

157 *A photograph of Oxford Road looking towards Valley Road, taken on 28 October 1959. Even in the early 1960s Oxford Road was still being spoken of as a 'rural retreat near the heart of Clacton'. It was one of the areas that was later turned into an industrial estate to try and ameliorate the problems caused by the collapsing holiday trade.*

158 *As one sign of Clacton's resurgence in the 1990s, the Punch & Judy returned to the beach under Peter Battey.*

159 *Clacton Shopping Village has helped bring the crowds back to Clacton.*

renaissance, both economically and as a holiday centre. First, in 1998, an entire new shopping village, Clacton Common, was opened within the old village boundary and, secondly, in 2001 one of Clacton's largest caravan parks, Highfields, also falling within the old village boundary, was expanded to accommodate up to 50,000 visitors a year. As a sign of the re-establishment of Clacton, and especially

the old village, St John's has re-opened for services following a ten-year closure.

It is probably true to say that Clacton-on-Sea will never again see the numbers of holidaymakers that were arriving in the '20s, '30s and '50s and many of the facilities will never return. But there is also no doubt that Clacton has managed to re-establish itself as a popular resort for day and weekend visitors, if not for weekly holidays. It still retains two theatres and one cinema. The pier and the Band Pavilion still provide typical seaside amusements. There is Magic City, an indoor entertainment centre for children. The Vista Road Recreation Ground and Sports Hall has expanded in recent years and provides much in the way of sporting facilities. There are still the beautifully laid-out gardens behind the three miles of golden sand and Peter Bruff's original plan for the centre of Clacton still provides a shopping centre with wide streets and a feeling of light and space.

As the song goes, 'things can only get better'. Welcome to Sunny Clacton!

Bibliography

Allen, C. J., *The Great Eastern Railway*, 1955

Baker, T., *Clacton-on-Sea in Old Picture Postcards*, Vols. 1 and 2, 1984 and 1992

Banks, I., *Rails to Jaywick Sands*, 1988

Box, P., *Belles of the East Coast*, 1989

Box, P., *Paddle Steamers of the Thames*, 2000

Bridgland, D.R. et al, 'Middle Pleistocene interglacial Thames–Medway deposits at Clacton-on-Sea', *Quaternary Science Reviews 18*, 1999

Butlin, Sir B., *The Billy Butlin Story*, 1982

Clacton & District Local History Society, *Town Walk*, 1989 (reprinted 2000)

Clacton & District Local History Society, *Newsletter and Clacton Chronicle*, 1985–1997

Clacton Gazette, *Clacton Then & Now*, 1996

Cole, M.A., *Holiday Camp Mystery*, 1959

Darvill, T., *Prehistoric Britain*, 1997

Essam, B. and Freeman, P., *Bricks and Rollers*, 1994

Froom, J., *A Century of Valour*, 1978

Grieve, H., *The Great Tide*, 1959

Hardwick, G., *Paper Clips*, c.1990

Hermon, E., *St Osyth Road School, A Centenary Celebration*, 1994

Jacobs, N., *Clacton in Camera*, 1984

Jacobs, N., *The Sunshine Coast*, 1986

Jacobs, N., *Clacton-on-Sea: A Pictorial History*, 1993

Jacobs, N., *West Cliff Story*, 1994

Jacobs, N., *Images of England, Clacton-on-Sea*, 2000

Jacobs, N., *Clacton-on-Sea, a photographic history of your town*, 2001

Karn, Valerie A., *Retiring to the Seaside*, 1977

Kennell, R., *From Little Holland to Holland-on-Sea*, 2000

Lyons, M., *The Story of Jaywick Sands Estate*, 1996

Morris, J., *Story of the Clacton-on-Sea Lifeboats*, 1991

North, R., *The Butlin Story*, 1962

Phillips, C., *The Tendring Hundred Railway*, 1989

Polley, B., *The Ramblas*, 1993

Read, S., *Hello Campers*, 1986

Rouse, M., *Coastal Resorts of East Anglia*, 1982

Skudder, J.M., 'The Seaside Resort as a Business Venture', *Essex Archaeology and History*, Volume 16, 1984-5

Walker, K., *The History of Clacton*, 1966

Walker, K., 'Clacton's Centenary', *Essex Journal*, Volume 6, No. 3, 1971

Walker, K., *Britain in Old Photographs, Clacton-on-Sea*, 1995

Ward, C. and Hardy, D., *Arcadia for All*, 1984

Ward, C. and Hardy, D., *Goodnight Campers*, 1986

Index

Page numbers in **bold** refer to illustrations

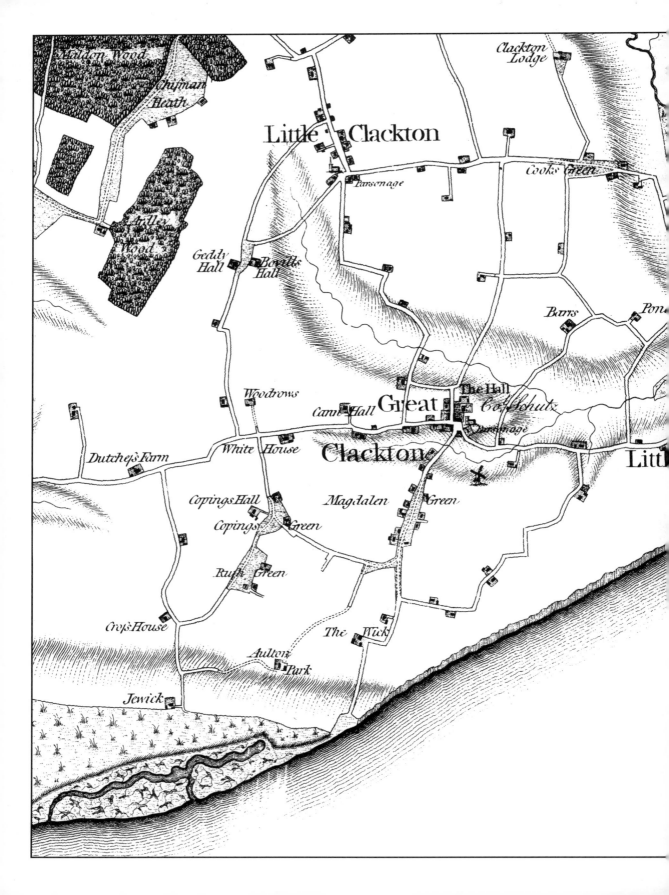

Milden Wood

Chipman Heath

Arley Wood

Little Clackton

Clackton Lodge

Cooks Green

Parsonage

Geddy Hall

Bovills Hall

Barrs

Pon

Woodrows

Carne Hall

Great

The Hall

Co:Schutz

Parsonage

Dutches Farm

White House

Clackton

Litt

Copings Hall

Magdalen

Green

Copings Green

Rush Green

Crofs House

The Wick

Aulton Park

Jewick